UNDERCOVER
WAR

BRITAIN'S SPECIAL FORCES
AND THEIR BATTLE AGAINST THE IRA

HARRY
McCALLION

JOHN BLAKE

Published by John Blake Publishing,
an imprint of Bonnier Books UK
80–81 Wimple Street
London
W1G 9RE

www.facebook.com/johnblakebooks
twitter.com/jblakebooks

First published in paperback in 2020

Paperback: 978 1 78946 285 2
Ebook: 978 1 78946 334 7

British Library Cataloguing-in-Publication Data:

A catalogue record for this book is available from the British Library.

Cover design by www.envydesign.co.uk

Printed and bound in Great Britain by Clays Ltd, Elcograf S.p.A.

3 5 7 9 10 8 6 4 2

John Blake Publishing is an imprint of Bonnier Books UK

www.bonnierbooks.co.uk

UNDERCOVER
WAR

This book is dedicated to the memory of

Sergeant Paul Oram MM
and Sergeant Alistair Slater MM

Two warriors who made the ultimate sacrifice for their
regiments, their country, and peace in Northern Ireland

CONTENTS

GLOSSARY

ASU	Active Service Unit
CESA	Catholic Ex-Servicemen's Association
CIA	Central Intelligence Agency
CIRA	Continuity Irish Republican Army
CQB	Close Quarter Battle
DCM	Distinguished Conduct Medal
DPP	Director of Public Prosecutions
DSO	Distinguished Service Order
DUP	Democratic Unionist Party
FBI	Federal Bureau of Investigation
FRU	Force Research Unit
GC	George Cross
GFA	Good Friday Agreement
HMSU	Headquarters Mobile Support Unit
INLA	Irish National Liberation Army
IPLO	Irish People's Liberation Organisation
IRA	Irish Republican Army

KOSB	King's Own Scottish Borderers
MLA	Member of the (Northern Ireland) Legislative Assembly
MLO	Military Intelligence Liaison Officer
MM	Military Medal
MoD	Ministry of Defence
MP	Military Police
MRF	Military Reaction Force
NCO	non-commissioned officer
NILA	Northern Ireland Legislative Assembly
NIRA	New Irish Republican Army
NITAT (NI)	Northern Ireland Training and Advisory Teams (Northern Ireland)
NYPD	New York Police Department
OIRA	Official Irish Republican Army
OP	observation post
PIRA	Provisional Irish Republican Army
PSNI	Police Service of Northern Ireland (*see also* RUC)
RIRA	Real Irish Republican Army
RSM	Regimental Sergeant Major
RTUd	Returned to Unit

RUC	Royal Ulster Constabulary (*see also* PSNI)
SAS	Special Air Service
SBS	Special Boat Service
SDLP	Social Democratic and Labour Party
SLR	Self-Loading Rifle
SOE	Special Operations Executive
SOP	Standard Operating Procedure
SRR	Special Reconnaissance Regiment
SRU	Special Reconnaissance Unit
SSU	Special Support Unit
TCG	Tasking and Co-ordination Group
UDA	Ulster Defence Association
UDR	Ulster Defence Regiment
UUP	Ulster Unionist Party
UVF	Ulster Volunteer Force
VCP	vehicle checkpoint
WIU	Weapons Intelligence Unit
WTC	World Trade Center

CHAPTER ONE

THE BEGINNING

THE MRF

When the first units of the British Army deployed to Northern Ireland in August 1969, they were completely unprepared for the maelstrom of violence that was about to engulf the province. Uniformed soldiers who were trained to stand against the armies of the Warsaw Pact instead found themselves in the middle of a bitter sectarian conflict. Rather than fighting Soviet tanks on the open plains of North Germany, they faced enemies who fought from the shadows, hiding themselves among the civilian population and only breaking cover when they were ready to attack.

Initial attempts to pursue a covert war against this foe were an unmitigated disaster. Incompetence, short-sightedness and murderous ill-discipline handed a propaganda coup to the enemy. The British Army's reputation was damaged for decades and these early failures helped entrench the power of the militant organisations, ultimately prolonging the conflict in Ulster. It was only with the deployment of professionally trained undercover units some years later that the British security services were able to undo these early mistakes and take the war to the terrorists with deadly efficiency.

The first British covert unit to be established in Northern Ireland was the Military Reaction Force (MRF). Between 1970 and 1972, the senior British officer in Belfast was Brigadier Frank Kitson. Kitson's early career had been spent suppressing colonial independence movements in the aftermath of the Second World War. The experiences he gained and the books he wrote on the subject led to him being seen in military circles as an important authority on the subject of fighting insurgents.

While the exact origins of the MRF are hazy, the unit's operating philosophy seems to have been based on Kitson's experiences fighting the Mau Mau in Kenya during the early 1950s.* Kitson viewed insurgents as 'gangs' who were both separate from the wider population yet at the same time relied on them for support. His strategy was to create 'counter-gangs' of his own to infiltrate the enemy and identify key members for arrest. Although these counter-gangs were officially intended as an intelligence-gathering tool, Kitson also noted in his writings the importance of controlling and manipulating the wider population to deny insurgents a support

---

* Kitson, F., *Gangs and Counter-Gangs*, 1960. While the details of the formal founding of the MRF remain unknown, General Sir Mike Jackson reports in his book *Soldier* (2007) that Kitson was 'the sun around which the planets revolved, and he very much set the tone for the operational style' in his region (p. 82).

base.* These two goals were combined to disastrous effect in the MRF. While Brigadier Kitson's tactics may have been successful against unsophisticated post-colonial insurgencies, they were to prove almost completely ineffective against a well-organised European terrorist group like the Provisional IRA (PIRA).

The MRF was based at a fenced-off compound within Palace Barracks, in the north Belfast suburb of Holywood. Officially, the MRF was a company-level establishment commanded by a captain (initially, Captain Arthur Watchus, then, later, Captain James McGregor); however, the unit operated entirely outside the normal chain of command, working as an independent asset that answered directly to Kitson's Brigade HQ. This kind of unconventional command structure is not unusual for Special Forces units. However, the threat to military discipline it poses is normally tempered by institutional traditions and history. As an *ad hoc* unit created in the field, the MRF had no such restraints.

The MRF was structured around a core of regular operators drawn from a variety of regiments (serving members of the SAS and SBS – Special Air Service and Special Boat Service,

---

* Likening a gang to a fish and the wider population to the water it swims in, Kitson wrote: 'If a fish has got to be destroyed it can be attacked directly by rod or net, providing it is in the sort of position which gives these methods a chance of success. But if the rod and net cannot succeed by themselves it may be necessary to do something to the water which will force the fish into a position where it can be caught. Conceivably, it might be necessary to kill the fish by polluting the water …' *Low Intensity Operations,* 1971, p. 49. Further on, he writes, 'conditions can be made reasonably uncomfortable for the population as a whole in order to provide an incentive for a return to normal life and to act as a deterrent towards the resumption of the campaign' (p. 87).

respectively – were not permitted to join as these units were barred from Ulster at the time). To augment the permanent core, every battalion that deployed on a tour in the province was tasked to select four men to serve with the unit. The soldiers who were chosen received no special training and it was left to each unit to determine whether individual volunteers had suitable tempera-ments and skills for the job.

When they returned to their units, soldiers often spoke openly about their activities with the MRF. In 2 Para, for example, Paul 'I', Ian 'B' and Mick 'W' all talked freely about the unit's opera-tions to anybody who was willing to listen. Operators from other units were equally indiscrete and the MRF's activities in West Belfast soon became an open secret throughout the Army. Senior officers were certainly aware of the unit's behaviour but they either approved of the MRF's hardline tactics or deliberately ignored the growing evidence of its excesses.

Training within the MRF, such as it was, was conducted on the job. New operators were placed with more experienced members of the unit to learn the basics of surveillance, radio procedure and patrol tactics. Due to the *ad hoc* nature of the unit, MRF patrols had no clearly defined operational procedures, such as anti-ambush drills or immediate contact drills. Nor did opera-tors receive even the most basic training in urban or rural covert surveillance prior to deployment.

The MRF operated with no clear oversight from Britain's intelligence agencies or from the Royal Ulster Constabulary (RUC). The RUC in the early 1970s was in a state of complete disarray as it struggled to adapt to the spiralling violence in Ulster. RUC Special Branch, in particular, was understaffed and unprepared to deal with the resurgent IRA. Given the lack of resources and manpower, the idea of focusing what little was available on investigating a British military unit would have been inconceivable. MI5 and MI6 were focused at the time on the ongoing Cold War against the Soviet Union and they too had been caught flatfooted by the escalating conflict in the province. Neither organisation provided any significant input into MRF operations and nor were they able to act as a brake or stabilising force on the behaviour of the unit.

In short, the MRF was a poorly trained and poorly disciplined unit operating in civilian clothes on deniable missions and entirely outside the normal chain of command. They answered only to a senior staff headed by a specialist in colonial counter-insurgency and they believed themselves to be beyond the reach of the law. This was a perfect storm of the kind of circumstances that could allow a military unit to go rogue.

What limited oversight there was of MRF activities came from the Army's own Military Police. This was purely nominal. After a 'contact', MPs would take statements from the operators involved. The operators' accounts were accepted without reservation or question, and the MPs would often rewrite the statements to make them appear more legally 'sound'. In particular, when MRF operators used lethal force, there was no scrutiny as to whether their actions were really justified under the Rules of Engagement that were supposed to guide soldiers deployed in the province.

Mick 'W', who spent a four-month tour seconded to the MRF, described one 'debriefing' as follows:

> When Taff Williams [Sergeant Clive Graham Williams, a military policeman seconded full-time to the MRF] told the debriefing NCO that he had had a contact, the NCO's response was "Not another kill, Sergeant Williams? Best tell me all about it." Williams then recounted how he had shot a 15-year-old boy in Andersonstown in West Belfast. Williams claimed [that the boy] was walking down the street carrying an M1 carbine.

Whether this is an accurate account of the conversation or contains elements of exaggeration is impossible to say. However, the details certainly fit with the pattern of behaviour that was common at the time. No questions were asked to determine whether there was any truth to the claim. Even following the death of a minor, the automatic assumption was that the reported circumstances were legitimate. Sergeant Williams went on to become the most notorious killer in the MRF.

The main operational problem the MRF faced was a complete lack of proper source intelligence. Neither MI5 nor Special Branch had informants inside the newly formed and ruthless Provisional IRA. The little intelligence that the security forces possessed was woefully out of date. This limitation was highlighted when police and soldiers attempted to implement the government's new policy of internment in August 1971. Most of the individuals arrested were either not involved in the current terrorist organisations or were past members of the less-violent Official IRA. Accurate information that could be used to direct targeted operations was almost entirely absent. In pursuing their own covert war, the MRF were thus operating almost entirely blind.

MRF attempts at gathering their own intelligence were extremely rudimentary. Low-level informers picked up off the streets were sometimes driven through republican areas and told to point out anyone they thought was a terrorist. Unsurprisingly, the quality of information gained in this way was very poor. MRF operators also tried to infiltrate the areas themselves by posing as in-offensive visitors, such as drunks or rubbish collectors, in the hope of identifying suspicious behaviour. One such attempt was recounted to the author by Ian 'B', a former member of the unit. Ian, together with another operator – who was on secondment from the Welsh Guards – entered a bookmaker's shop in West Belfast wearing civilian clothes and posing as punters. A pre-arranged 'hard search' was then conducted by an Army patrol in order to allow the MRF operators to observe reactions and to hear what was said by the locals in the shop. The 'operation', if we can call it that, was blown as soon as the search team left. The seconded Guardsman turned to the man standing next to him and asked in a loud Welsh accent, 'Does this happen often, Boyo?' The surprising presence of a clue-less, inquisitive Welshman in the immediate aftermath of a British Army raid was more than enough to make the locals suspicious.

Fortunately, Ian 'B' managed to extract himself and his companion from the suddenly hostile environment before an IRA Active Service Unit (ASU) could arrive to 'investigate' further.

According to at least one MRF operator, the unit also abducted suspects from the streets and interrogated them for information. Some operators are reported to have used brutal methods to coerce abductees into cooperating. The interrogation would start with the operators breaking one of the suspect's arms. Having made clear the lengths to which they were willing to go, they would then threaten to break the other arm unless information was forthcoming.* Once the interrogation was over, the abductee would be 'dropped […] off at the roadside for the uniformed forces to pick up later'.†

More serious attempts at intelligence-gathering were made using business fronts, including the Four Square Laundry, and also

---

* This casual attitude to the abuse of prisoners may have been informed by the attitude of Brigadier Kitson himself. In his *Gangs and Counter-Gangs*, Kitson condemns the use of torture in a passage dripping with sarcasm: 'And so it came about that, once in a way, somebody would take the law into his own hands and strike a blow where one seemed necessary, because the existing legal methods of dealing with the situation were not good enough. Looking back, I am sure that this was wrong. Certainly this sort of conduct saved countless loyalist lives and shortened the Emergency. All the same it was wrong because the good name of Britain was being lost for the sake of saving a few thousand Africans and a few million pounds of the taxpayers' money.'

† MRF operator Simon Cursey, talking to the *Mail on Sunday* (22 December 2012). Cursey is the author of a book *MRF Shadow Troop* about his time in the MRF that skirts around the activities of the unit. Only in Chapter 12 does he come close to giving a true account of the behaviour the MRF engaged in, although it is dressed up as a hypothetical discussion about what the unit would have done if they were given permission to follow their own instincts.

the Gemini Massage Parlour on Antrim Road. A Four Square van visited houses in nationalist West Belfast twice a week to collect and deliver laundry, winning over new customers by handing out discount vouchers that were numbered and colour-coded by street. One operator drove the van while another, a woman, collected and delivered the laundry. All the clothes collected for washing were checked forensically for traces of explosives, as well as for blood or firearms residue. A roof compartment in the van also served as a mobile observation post when needed.

The laundry provided an excellent service at discount prices and it quickly built up a strong client base. However, the operation was fatally flawed by a lack of attention to detail. While the 'delivery van' looked the part, with a contact number displayed prominently on its side, no one thought to set up an answering service. Whenever a resident attempted to call the laundry to discuss a delivery, they were met with a suspicious lack of response. This information soon found its way to the PIRA, who quickly concluded that the business was a front for intelligence-gathering.

On 2 October 1972, Provisional IRA volunteers ambushed the Four Square Laundry van in the nationalist Twinbrook area of Belfast, shooting dead the driver, Tedford Stuart. The PIRA team also machine-gunned the roof compartment, where they suspected that undercover operatives were hiding. The female operator present that day was fortunate enough to be collecting laundry from a nearby house at the time. The residents, who thought the van was under attack by loyalist terrorists, took her into the house and kept her safe. Ted Stuart, a native of Northern Ireland from

Strabane who was detached to the MRF from the Royal Engineers, was the only member of the unit to be killed in action.

The Gemini Massage Parlour on Antrim Road was also attacked by the Provisional IRA's 3rd Battalion. The PIRA unit responsible claimed they killed a number of undercover soldiers during the operation. This is untrue. The MRF suffered no casualties in the attack as no operators were present in the building that day.

Two Provisional IRA volunteers were subsequently killed on the orders of PIRA commanders and secretly buried in the Republic of Ireland. The PIRA claimed the pair were agents of the MRF and that the Four Square Laundry operation was discovered as a result of their interrogation. Whether or not these men were in fact 'agents of the MRF', the author cannot say. But they were certainly not the reason that the operation was blown.

In addition to intelligence-gathering, the second, far more controversial, role of the MRF was to proactively drive around republican areas of Belfast in search of terrorists. Nearly all the unit's operators grew beards and wore their hair long in order to blend in with the local civilian population. They patrolled in plainclothes, three or four men to a car, 'looking for trouble'. These operations were both ineffective and poorly coordinated. On one occasion, two MRF patrols in the Springfield Road area shot at each other, each believing that the other car full of suspiciously watchful men contained a terrorist ASU.

While the MRF patrols may, at times, have had trouble identifying each other, the PIRA had no such problems. Shaggy hair notwithstanding, a car full of fit, hard-looking, unfamiliar men stuck out like a sore thumb in the clannish republican communities. One MRF operator gave the following account of a contact to the BBC's *Panorama*:

> When I had my first operation there were three of us in this clapped out Avenger and I was the back seat rider. We saw a car on the wanted list and we turned round and all of a sudden they were behind us. At that time my own personal weapon was the Browning 9mm. All of a sudden they open up with an Armalite.

The car was riddled with bullets but none of the operators were hit.

Operating in this way, the MRF killed a large number of people who they subsequently claimed were terrorists. Many, in fact, were unarmed civilians. Among the documented shootings that can be attributed to the MRF is the killing of two brothers, Gerry and John Conway. Gerry and John were both shot by a three-man MRF patrol on 15 April 1972 while walking along Whiterock Road to catch a bus. An official Army statement claimed that the patrol had encountered two wanted men, that one had fired at the patrol, and that the soldiers then returned fire. In June 1978, a man claiming to be a former MRF operator spoke at a Troops Out Movement meeting in Bristol. He admitted that he had been one of the gunmen and confirmed that the two brothers were unarmed. Gerry and John had apparently been mistaken for two IRA men who were on the MRF's 'shoot on sight' list.

On 12 May 1972, MRF teams carried out a number of shootings in the Andersonstown area of West Belfast. Two Catholic civilians, Aidan McAloon and Eugene Devlin, were shot by MRF operators in a civilian car as they walked towards a barricade set up by a local 'self-defence' organisation. When making their statements to the Military Police, the operators reported that they had shot at a man who was not only armed but was firing a rifle.

One of the MRF men present recounted a rather different version of events to the author. As the unmarked car drove down the road, an operator inside claimed to have seen an armed man at the barricade. The team made several further passes in an attempt to confirm the sighting of a weapon but they were unable to identify a gunman. Nevertheless, they decided to give the barricade 'a spray' on their final pass and it was this volley that hit McAloon and Devlin.

Indiscriminately spraying barricades with gunfire was common in the MRF, as a former operator revealed to a *Panorama* investigation team. Another operator wrote about the illegal tactic in a hypothetical voice so as not to incriminate himself:

> But late at night if we came across manned barricades, masked vigilante patrols or suspicious groups milling about in the most dangerous notorious areas and streets, we could possibly initiate a contact. The idea was, we'd make a pass, checking them over, then perhaps open fire and let them have a short burst of four or five rounds from our SMG [submachine gun].

The justification for breaking the formal rules of engagement was that such groups were *always up to no good* and would hide their weapons as soon as they were approached by uniformed soldiers or police.

> As far as we were concerned these people were just as guilty as the most hardened terrorists [sic] gunmen or bombers [...] Types such as these probably didn't have the balls to go out and join an IRA Active Service Unit but they were nonetheless sympathisers and supporters, assisting the movement.*

This kind of disastrous thinking ran through everything the MRF did. It not only stained the British Army's operations in Ulster but also gave the PIRA a vital propaganda resource. Later lies about SAS policies in Northern Ireland were given a veneer of plausibility by the very real actions of the MRF in the early 1970s. These stories were to provide the PIRA with a valuable recruiting tool. They directly helped to sustain the terrorist organisation by fanning the flames of hatred against the British security forces and, in doing so, contributed to the prolongation of the Troubles.

For the Catholics of Andersonstown on 12 May 1972, the danger was much more immediate. Just minutes after the shooting of McAloon and Devlin, an MRF car approached another checkpoint at the entrance to Riverdale Park South. This checkpoint was manned by members of the Catholic Ex-Servicemen's Association (CESA), an unarmed vigilante organisation set up to protect Catholic areas from loyalist violence. The MRF car

---

* Simon Cursey, 2013, *MRF: Shadow Troop*, pp. 219–20.

stopped in front of the barricade and then reversed. As they backed away, one of the MRF men opened fire from the car with a submachine gun, killing Catholic civilian Patrick McVeigh (44) and wounding four others. The car finished reversing, turned and then drove away past the scene of the shooting.

All of the victims were local residents. McVeigh, who was shot through the back, had stopped to chat to the CESA members as he walked home. He was a married father of six children and was given the Last Rites at the scene by a local priest. An official Army statement released after the shooting blamed the attack on loyalist gunmen and described the killing as an 'apparently motiveless crime'. An inquest into McVeigh's death was held in December 1972, during the course of which evidence revealed that the car's occupants were operators from the MRF. The soldiers did not appear at the inquest but issued statements to it claiming they had been shot at by six gunmen and were returning fire. However, eyewitnesses deny this and no traces of gun residue were found on the victims' clothes.

Almost two weeks later, on 27 May 1972, Catholic civilian Gerard Duddy (20) was killed on almost exactly the same spot Patrick McVeigh had been standing when he was shot. At the time of Duddy's death, the attack was blamed on loyalist paramilitaries but this was, in fact, another MRF drive-by shooting.

On the night of 9 June 1972, Catholic civilian Jean Smyth (24), a mother of one, was shot dead on the Glen Road while sitting in the passenger seat of a car near the bus terminus. The male driver had pulled the car over when he heard what he thought was a tyre bursting. As the driver got out to check, the car was hit by automatic gunfire. Jean Smyth was shot in the head and died shortly afterwards. The security forces blamed the killing on the IRA. In October 1973, however, the *Belfast Telegraph* published an article suggesting that Smyth might have been shot by the MRF. MRF units had been in the area that night and reported that they had opened fire while on patrol. In their report, they claimed to have shot at two gunmen, hitting one of them.

On 22 June 1972, MRF operator Sergeant 'Taff' Williams machine-gunned a group of three Catholic men standing by a car very close to where Jean Smyth had been killed. Williams used a Thompson submachine gun in the shooting, a weapon favoured by the IRA. A man in a nearby house was also wounded by the gunfire. Shortly afterwards, the MRF unit's car was stopped by the RUC and the occupants were arrested.

In a rare instance of an MRF operator being held to some sort of account for his actions, Williams was prosecuted for attempted murder. He told the court that two of the men had been armed and that one had fired at the patrol car, claiming that he was simply returning fire at hostile gunmen. Witnesses stated that none of the civilians were armed and that the attack was unprovoked. Police forensics experts found no evidence that the civilians had fired any weapons. Nevertheless, Williams was acquitted.

Former MRF operator Mick 'W' informed the author of this book that, to his firm knowledge, Williams had killed at least 15 people in Northern Ireland. Williams was a decorated soldier who had been awarded a Military Medal for foiling a bank robbery.

The respect he received for this decoration meant that he was given even more latitude than other MRF soldiers. Mick 'W' described him as 'a psycho with an MM'.

Daniel Rooney (18) was killed by soldiers from the MRF on 27 September 1972. He was shot on St James' Crescent, close to his home in Rodney Parade in West Belfast, and died shortly afterwards in hospital. A statement from the Army claimed that five shots were fired at a security force surveillance patrol in the St James' Park area and that fire was returned. The official Army line was that Rooney was a known gunman but the IRA have never acknowledged him as a member and he is listed on a memorial as a civilian. His clothes were forensically tested by the RUC and no trace of gun residue was found. The six MRF operators involved in the shooting did not appear at the inquest. Their statements were read by an RUC officer and they were referred to by letters. The MRF operators claimed that Rooney and his companion were carrying a rifle and a handgun.

Some reports have asserted that the MRF collaborated with loyalist terrorist groups but the author has found no evidence to corroborate this claim. However, what is not in dispute is that many of the MRF's shootings in West Belfast were blamed on loyalist paramilitaries. This inevitably led to retaliation from republican terrorist groups against Protestant civilians and counter-retaliation by loyalists against Catholics.

The debacle of the Four Square Laundry operation and the resulting death of an MRF operator brought the unit's operations into sharp focus for the British Army's high command. Senior officers at last began to take seriously accounts of the MRF's questionable behaviour. In the wake of the spate of drive-by killings, the RUC had also begun to investigate the unit's activities. There was an increasing unwillingness at all levels and across all services to let an ill-disciplined, poorly controlled and ultimately ineffective unit run roughshod over proper procedures, not to mention human decency. The prosecution of Taff Williams was the last straw for the Army, who realised they had a ticking time-bomb on their hands.

A decision was taken to immediately disband the MRF. The unit had been in existence for just 18 months but had done untold damage. The total number of people killed by the MRF will never be known. However, anecdotal evidence combined with the facts in the public record suggest that at least 40 civilians lost their lives at the hands of what can best be described as a legalised murder gang. The activities of the MRF were a stain on the reputation of the British Army and provided an invaluable propaganda and recruitment tool to the IRA. Their legacy was the creation of an unbridgeable lack of trust between nationalists and the British Army, a situation that was to last throughout the Troubles.

The demise of the MRF left the Army with no covert surveillance unit to combat the increasingly sophisticated campaigns of the republican and loyalist terror organisations. Secret talks in early 1972 between the British government and the IRA had ended in failure, and 1972 went on to become the single most violent year of the Troubles in Northern Ireland. In one year, the Army and the RUC suffered 149 fatalities, with hundreds more wounded. Civilian deaths reached a high of 249.

The Army's own intelligence services knew that the Provisional IRA were making plans for a 'long war', with the intent to grind down Britain's resolve to stay in Northern Ireland. An effective covert capability was now a necessity. With no other options, British senior commanders turned to the one unit in the Army capable of carrying out the task: the 22nd Special Air Service Regiment.

CHAPTER TWO

INCOGNITO

THE FIRST DEPLOYMENT OF THE SAS

In the vacuum left by the disbandment of the MRF, the British Army's senior officers in Northern Ireland were faced with a complete lack of available units with a specialised covert surveillance capability. The only unit in the Army that possessed the necessary expertise was the SAS but the Government's position at the time was that the deployment of Special Forces soldiers to Northern Ireland would undermine the official line that republican terrorists were nothing more than criminals. Government ministers gave repeated assurances in Parliament that such forces were not, and would not be, engaged in the growing turmoil in the province. Such a move, it was felt, would amount to an acknowledgement that the situation had escalated to the level of all-out warfare. It has become a commonplace these days to assume that politicians cannot be trusted but, at the time, breaking such a firm commitment and deliberately misleading Parliament was an unthinkable step.

To get around this seemingly intractable situation, the Army came up with a simple, if somewhat devious, solution. Since 1971, the SAS had been heavily engaged in a covert conflict in Oman, codenamed Operation Storm, where they were fighting an undeclared war against an insurgency in the province of Dhofar. The most notable battle of the war took place on 19 July 1972, at an isolated hill fort called Mirbat. Here, nine members of B Squadron fought off a concerted attack by hundreds of heavily-armed rebels. Two members of the squadron, Thomas Tobin and the redoubtable Fijian warrior Talaiasi Labalaba, were killed in the battle. Four of the survivors were decorated for valour, with a Distinguished Service Order, a Distinguished Conduct Medal and two Military Medals.

It was to the men of B Squadron that the Army turned in order to bridge the surveillance gap in Northern Ireland. In 1973, the squadron was taken out of the normal regimental rotation. Half its men were given the task of recruiting and training a new unit to replace the now-defunct MRF. The other half of the squadron was officially de-badged, or removed from the SAS rolls and returned to their original units. These men, technically no longer members of the Special Forces, were then posted together to Ulster in a covert surveillance role.*

---

* The British government was fully aware of the Army's actions, as is made clear in a Top Secret briefing to the Prime Minister from 1974, entitled 'Defensive Brief D – Meeting between the Prime Minister and the Taoiseach, 5 April 1974, Army Plain Clothes Patrols in Northern Ireland'.

To say this deployment caused consternation within the SAS would be a gross understatement. Many serving members had specifically joined the regiment in order to avoid tours of duty in Ulster, where they faced an unseen, intractable enemy, hidden within a hostile civilian population and impossible to get to grips with in straightforward combat. Most soldiers in regular regiments considered the 'Yellow Card' rules of engagement to be unduly restrictive and felt that, while on patrol, they were able to do little more than provide target practice for the IRA's gunmen. Among the soldiers of the SAS, the distaste for what was seen as political interference was even more intense. Given the choice between a tour in Ulster and a tour in Dhofar, most SAS troopers would have chosen Dhofar any day of the week and twice on Sundays, despite the discomforts and dangers of combat under the Arabian sun.

Those members of B Squadron assigned to the 'de-badged' group were also acutely aware that the entire operation was deniable. If they were killed in action, their names would not appear on the SAS Roll of Honour and their service with the SAS would be denied. For soldiers who had passed the rigours of SAS selection and made the regiment their home, this was far from a negligible concern. For many members, the regiment was family and to be cut off from the family name, even if only on paper, felt like losing a limb. Despite the reservations of the men involved, the Army considered the operation to be vital and B Squadron had no choice but to rise to the challenge.

The half-squadron sent to Ulster spent some four weeks in training, honing their already considerable skills in urban and rural covert surveillance. Once deployed, the de-badged soldiers took over the old MRF compound in Holywood and began the work of familiarising themselves with their new environment. In this endeavour, the recently reformed and now much more professional RUC Special Branch provided vital assistance. Close personal links were formed between the two units that were to prove invaluable in the future.

Special Branch briefed the SAS team on the Provisional IRA's command structure, which in 1973 was still based around the quasi-military formations of brigades, battalions and companies. The Belfast Brigade, for example, had three battalions, based, respectively, in the Andersonstown, Lenadoon and Suffolk area, Ballymurphy and the Falls, and the Ardoyne and New Lodge Road areas in the north of the city. The men were also briefed on the modes of operation of the different terrorist units, as well as on their weapons and tactics. MI5 agent handlers, who had by this time begun to infiltrate informers into both republican and loyalist paramilitary organisations, also briefed the team. In contrast to the earlier MRF era, when the SAS began an operation they made sure they were acting on reliable source intelligence.

In January 1974, SAS teams began covert operations against known Provisional IRA members operating in County Down. Their initial main focus was on tracking an individual who Special Branch believed to be the local PIRA quartermaster. On a number of occasions, surveillance teams followed the suspect as he travelled to a forested area near the village of Rostrevor. Given the frequency of his visits and the unusual location, the

SAS teams concluded that an arms dump was located some-where in the vicinity. In order to find it, they called in a local army unit from the Welsh Guards to conduct an area search of some 20 acres of forestry. Careful examination of every nook and cranny of the terrain led to a number of separate finds. In the first, the Guards uncovered camouflage suits and a .303 rifle concealed in a rabbit burrow. A second hide, found some miles away, yielded 200 detonators, 1,800 feet of detonating cord and 75lbs of homemade explosives. But it was the third cache that proved most important. There, alongside bomb-making mate-rials and two mortar rounds, the search team discovered docu-mentation that definitively tied the quartermaster to the arms dumps and ultimately led to his arrest.

Later that month, teams from the half-squadron carried out a covert surveillance operation on a derelict farmhouse near Saint-field, County Down. Special Branch had identified the building as a possible weapons cache used by Protestant paramilitaries. An initial covert search revealed a Spanish 9mm Star semi-automatic pistol and large quantities of stolen consumer goods. With the source intelligence confirmed as good, an observation post (OP) was put in to watch the house in the hope of catching any terrorists who might visit the arms dump. For three days, the SAS teams lay in wait, with two men inside the farmhouse and four more in the concealed OP outside. On the night of 26 January, their patience paid off when a car containing four men pulled up outside the building. One of the occupants, William Black, got out of the vehicle and removed a rifle from the boot. He then entered the main building and began to make his way up the stairs, where he was confronted by the two SAS men waiting inside. On seeing the threat, Black raised his rifle and was promptly shot in the chest with a suppressed Sterling submachine gun.

The light 9mm rounds, travelling with less power than usual due to the suppressor on the soldier's weapon, failed to drop the target. The wounded man turned and fled into the darkness, running to a neighbouring farm, from where he was taken to hospital. The SAS team in the OP at the front of the building apprehended the other three members of the terrorist group and then called in regular Army search teams. A comprehensive inspection of the farmhouse revealed two further rifles and a quantity of ammunition. Black has the dubious honour of being the first man to be shot by the SAS in the Ulster Troubles. Few of those who followed him would be fortunate enough to live to tell the tale.

The SAS teams now turned their focus to the Belfast Brigade of the PIRA, and specifically to the goal of locating and capturing Ivor Bell, the Brigade Commander. The Belfast Brigade was the PIRA's most active unit and Bell was its fifth commander in five years. Billy McKee, the first holder of the post and one of the founding members of the PIRA, was arrested in 1971. He was replaced first by Joe Cahill, who fled south to avoid British internment four months later, and then by Seamus Twomey, who was subsequently promoted to Chief of Staff on the PIRA's ruling Army Council. The next commander of the brigade was Gerry Adams, who held the position briefly until his internment in July 1973. He was followed in the role by Bell, his second-in-command.

Unsurprisingly, given the rapid turnover of his predecessors, Bell was a very security-conscious individual. He ordered that all photographs of him should be destroyed and, unlike previous commanders, refused to have any contact at all with the press. He invented a new identity for himself, going by the name of Patrick McConnell, and took stringent anti-surveillance measures, switching houses and cars frequently in order to throw the security forces off the scent. These tactics worked as intended and made him a highly slippery and elusive target.

Working on information provided by Special Branch and MI5, the SAS slowly began to close the net around Bell. An intensive programme of mobile and foot surveillance was carried out, targeting known PIRA couriers. This methodical investigative work allowed the SAS to gradually identify a number of IRA safe houses around the city and then set up observation posts on each. Eventually, Bell was spotted, or 'housed', as the operators put it, at one of these locations. Local security forces were called in and, on 24 February 1974, Bell was arrested. The removal of yet another brigade commander seriously disrupted the PIRA's Belfast activities for several months.

A new commander, Brendan Hughes, took over the brigade and immediately became the next target of the SAS surveillance operation. From February to May 1974, the teams carried out intensive covert operations in West Belfast. The aim this time was not just to capture Hughes but to deal a significant blow to the brigade itself. Slowly but surely, the SAS teams pieced together a comprehensive picture of the Belfast Brigade's operational structure and behaviour.

On 10 May 1974, a series of raids were carried out across Belfast by regular Army units acting on the information supplied by the SAS. Brendan Hughes and his second-in-command, Dennis Loughran, were both arrested in an expensive house in the Myrtlefield area of the Malone Road in Belfast. Inside the £50,000 home (an enormous sum at a time when the average house cost just £5,000), the search teams found a complete attack plan for an impending general offensive, as well as arms, ammunition and 250 timing devices for bombs. Other raids the same day resulted in the discovery of significant arms finds in other parts of the city as well as the arrest of a leading PIRA gunman while he was standing in a dole queue. Follow-up operations, based on Special Branch's analysis of the information discovered in Myrtlefield, led to the seizing of 600lbs of explosives from a garage in Wellington Park.

This was the final major operation carried out by the SAS during the regiment's first, unofficial, deployment to the province. In a few short months, half a squadron of highly trained soldiers had proved the value of well-sourced covert operations, achieving successes that dwarfed anything the MRF had accomplished over nearly two years. The activities of the SAS teams severely disrupted the Provisional IRA, especially in Belfast, where the thwarting of a major offensive doubtless saved many civilian, army and police lives. But these achievements only marked the beginning of a new phase in the covert battle against the IRA. As the de-badged SAS men were withdrawn, happily returning home to their regimental family, they were replaced by another unit that would write its own page in the history of Britain's undercover war.

While one half of B Squadron was busy degrading the PIRA's capabilities in Ulster, the other half were engaged in the serious business of recruiting and training the new covert surveillance unit that would replace them. This unit went by a number of different cover names during its time in Northern Ireland and is most commonly referred to by its later official title of 14 Intelligence Company. To those working in the intelligence community in Northern Ireland, it came to be known simply as 'the Det'.*

In creating the Det, the SAS training team drew inspiration both from their own selection process and from that used by the Special Operations Executive (SOE) during the Second World War. Potential recruits, of whom the author was one, had first to pass a selection phase. This took place in a specially chosen, nearly deserted army barracks. Recruits were told to present themselves with no identification other than their army ID cards, which were confiscated immediately on arrival. Each recruit was then assigned a number in place of a name and was instructed never to reveal their real identity to any other recruit. All personal kit was then searched. Anyone who had disobeyed joining instructions

---

* Official documents from 1974 refer to the unit as the SRU (Special Reconnaissance Unit), noting that it operated at first under the cover name of Northern Ireland Training and Advisory Teams (Northern Ireland) (NITAT (NI)). This cover name mimicked the title of the real NITAT units that trained British troops for deployments to the province.

and brought identifying material with them was immediately RTUd (Returned to Unit).

Over the next two weeks, recruits were subjected to a combination of hard physical and mental tests, designed to ensure that they were not only fit enough for the role but were also able to think and make decisions when exhausted and under pressure. The physical tests included running, stretcher races (team races over rough ground or obstacle courses carrying a heavy stretcher) and 'milling', which involved spending three minutes in a boxing ring trying to knock the stuffing out of another recruit. The tests were conducted irregularly, at odd times of the day or night. Recruits might be woken up at 3 a.m. for a long run and then be assessed on their mental agility or tasked to undertake weapon training.

Weapons training and identification covered not only the weapons that were to be used by the future operators but also those fielded by the various terrorist organisations they would be operating against. Mental-agility tests were specifically designed to assess each recruit's aptitude for tasks related to covert surveillance. For instance, recruits might be placed in a darkened and apparently sealed room, then timed to see how long they took to find an exit. Another test involved sending recruits through a dimly-lit room and then examining them on what had been observed. Expectations were high and those who could not show the required level of detailed recall would be swiftly RTUd, regardless of their other qualities.

The mental tests were often combined with physical challenges. At the end of a run, recruits could be asked to describe the route they had taken and anything notable they had seen along the way. After an exhausting stretcher race, a recruit might be required to give a ten-minute lecture to an audience of instructors and then face questions from the training team. Those who survived the initial selection process proceeded to the training phase at Pontrilas in South Wales, half an hour down the road from the home of the SAS in Hereford.

The training at Pontrilas was intensive. Potential operators were no longer referred to by a number but had, instead, to choose a new name for themselves. This name remained with them for the entire time they served with the unit, their real identities protected even from those they worked alongside. Trainee operators were allowed to grow their hair long, as was fashionable in the seventies, and moustaches were also permitted. Beards, however, were strictly forbidden. The training teams believed that the complete lack of grooming standards in the MRF was a visible symbol of the indiscipline that led to the failure of the unit. Det operators, by contrast, were expected to remember at all times that they were an integrated part of the wider military structure. Rules concerning facial hair, minimal as they were, served to remind operators that working undercover did not mean they were free agents who could act however they wished.

Training concentrated on covert surveillance techniques, the setting up of static rural and urban OPs, and the mobile observation of suspects, both on foot and in vehicles. The mobile drills were often carried out in Hereford, a town full of highly alert off-duty SAS men, trained to spot any suspicious activity. This provided good practice for the hostile environment operators would face in both republican and loyalist areas of Ulster. Terrorist recognition was also a high priority. Future operators were taught a range of mental techniques to help them link a known 'face' to a name, as well as to assist in the recognition of cars and weapons.

Operators learned that following a single man on foot required at least three observers, two following behind the target and one on the opposite side of the street, all constantly switching positions in order to avoid detection. Car surveillance was even more complex. Anything up to six cars could be needed for a single target. As well as observing the suspect vehicle, operators also had to be able to navigate through the streets and use a concealed radio without looking like anything other than an ordinary driver.

Mundane tasks, such as attending a Catholic church service or placing a bet at a bookies, were practiced again and again to ensure that operators could behave naturally in any environment they were likely to encounter. Even something as simple as a bus journey required careful study. Since it was impossible to know in advance where a target might get off, operators learned to always pay a fixed fare and not to rely on the destination given on the front of the bus. On at least one occasion, an operator in the field had his cover blown when he tried to buy a ticket for the advertised destination only for the conductor to tell him that the bus actually served a different route. These were details any local would know, so trainee operators were taught to find ways around such gaps in their knowledge. They were also instructed to practice saying at least one specific phrase in a Northern Irish accent. If challenged while sitting in a car or standing on a street corner, every operator could convincingly answer 'I'm waiting for my girl', even if they couldn't carry on a longer conversation.

Another high priority was 'Close Quarter Battle' (CQB). Potential operators were extensively trained and drilled in the use of the Browning 9mm pistol, the workhorse weapon of the Det. The Browning was popular in both the SAS and the Det for its accuracy and reliability, and served as the standard pistol for both units throughout the Troubles. Operators learned to draw and fire from hip holsters and shoulder holsters (although the SAS instructors tended to disdain the use of such bulky equipment), as well as from holsters fixed to the inside of car doors for use in anti-ambush and anti-hijacking drills. Fast-draw techniques were learned and honed on the ranges of Pontrilas and in the SAS 'Killing House' at Bradbury Lines in Hereford.

Operators were taught to 'double tap', firing two rounds in quick succession at the main body mass of their target. This approach differed slightly from the CQB techniques used by the SAS. The SAS, and their anti-terrorist teams in particular, specifically trained for head shots because of the growing availability of body armour. Det operators, by contrast, were surveillance specialists and were not expected to have such highly developed skills in marksmanship. Nonetheless, by the end of their training, most operators could draw and hit a target in just over a second.

Customisation of the Browning was common. Both Det and SAS operators frequently used an extended 20 round magazine to provide additional firepower in a tight spot. Members of the Det would often fit enlarged safety-catches as well. When carried on operations, the pistol was always loaded and cocked. The speed with which an operator could begin getting rounds down on target was thus determined by how quickly he could switch the safety off. The larger safety catch also had the advantage of being easier to use with numb, rain-slicked fingers, a regular feature of working outside in Northern Ireland during the winter.

In addition to their pistol, all Det members also carried a 'car weapon' when on operations. Operators were instructed in the use of various submachine guns but the main car weapon was the American-made Ingram MAC-10, a squat compact machine pistol that was ideal for concealment but highly inaccurate when shooting at anything more than a few metres away. The SAS instructors disliked this extremely rapid-firing weapon, describing it as 'a very expensive way of turning 9mm rounds into empty cases'. However, due to its ability to spray a large number of rounds in a very short period of time, it remained the favoured backup weapon of 14 Intelligence Company operators, as well as members of the Special Boat Service (SBS), for many years. It was only in the 1980s, with the introduction of the much more accurate and reliable 'Kurz' (short) version of the Heckler & Koch MP5, that the MAC-10 finally fell out of favour with 14 Intelligence Company. The Kurz was slower-firing but far more accurate. The only drawback to the weapon was its extremely short barrel. In the heat of combat, soldiers would sometimes place the forefinger of their leading hand over the end of the barrel when they moved or steadied the weapon. During the Iranian Embassy siege in London in

1980, one SAS soldier actually shot the end of his finger off while firing a Kurz submachine gun. It was the only gunshot wound sustained by the regiment during the operation.

In the middle of the second Det selection course, on which the author was present, the unit received tragic news: on 14 April 1974, Captain Anthony Pollen, a former member of the Coldstream Guards, was killed on an operation in Londonderry. Captain Pollen was part of a four-man Det team that entered the Bogside area of Londonderry posing as journalists covering the traditional PIRA Easter Commemoration Parade. It was known that leading members of the Derry Brigade of the PIRA would be attending the parade, alongside a number of other notable IRA commanders, and Pollen's unit were there to observe them.

The team split into two pairs. One group, consisting of two corporals, kept its distance, while Captain Pollen and another corporal moved in and mingled with the crowd. For unknown reasons, their presence drew the attention of the PIRA 'marshals' responsible for keeping order and Pollen was directly challenged about his presence. When he was unable to provide satisfactory answers, the two operators became isolated as a crowd gathered in around them. Seeing the imminent danger, the corporal dashed away through a gap in the growing mass of bodies, shouting for the captain to follow. The corporal managed to link up with the other two operators and made good his escape. Captain Pollen was not so fortunate. Before he could get away, the crowd closed up, forming an impassable wall. The armed PIRA 'honour guard', who were present to fire a tribute volley in honour of the IRA's fallen, pushed their way through the crowd and shot him dead. Although he was armed, Captain Pollen did not draw his weapon and it was subsequently stolen from his body.

The incident was relayed to our course by the SAS CQB instructor, his face a mask of iron rage. After recounting in detail what had happened, he left the course with these words: '*There is a lesson to be learned from this. If in doubt, get it out. And, if you get it out, for damn's sake use it!*' The words were not lost on those present and the lesson was passed on to all future operators. Captain Pollen was the first member of 14 Intelligence Company to be killed in Northern Ireland. He would not be the last.

In addition to inspiring sage advice from the SAS instructors, Captain Pollen's tragic death also had a profound impact on the Standard Operating Procedures (SOPs) that informed 14 Intelligence Company's future operations. When working in urban areas, planned static OPs were, if possible, always provided with both a covering party and an immediate reaction force from the local army unit on standby. However, urban surveillance is, by its very nature, fluid. The reality of the situation often meant that OPs had to be set up at very short notice and in hostile areas where it was all but impossible to give the operators protection without also blowing their cover. In such circumstances, the operators were on their own and their main hope for survival lay in concealment.

My Det selection course was one of the last to be trained exclusively by the B Squadron team. As the experience-base of the unit developed, Det operators who had completed tours in the province gradually took over the instructor positions on the courses, although the SAS maintained a presence on the training staff. By this time, 14 Intelligence Company was fully operational and ready to carry the covert war right up to the doorsteps of Ulster's terrorist organisations.

CHAPTER THREE

HARD LESSONS

14 INTELLIGENCE COMPANY (1974–80)

The basic operating structure of 14 Intelligence Company in the 1970s was simple and effective. The unit was split into three detachments, or Dets, each assigned to one of the Army brigades responsible for security in the province. The Belfast and Mid Ulster Dets both operated out of an Army base in North Belfast, while the Londonderry Det operated from a secure compound in the heart of the city. Unlike the MRF, 14 Intelligence Company was part of the formal military command structure in the province. The provision of integrated support services served as critical 'force multipliers', enabling the Dets to carry out their surveillance activities efficiently and effectively.

Secure and reliable communications were vital to the success of covert operations throughout the undercover war. Accordingly, 14 Intelligence Company had its own dedicated signals unit, composed of hand-picked signallers who undertook a basic selection and training course at the company's training base in Pontrilas. Although the signals section of 14 Intelligence Company were not operators in the strict sense, they did, at times, have to work with operators in the field to maintain communications. In addition, there were many covert relay stations, some situated in army bases, some not, that required regular maintenance. This meant that covert signallers needed the skills to travel in civilian cars, often alone, to locations in hostile areas of Belfast and Londonderry.

As well as learning how to install and maintain specialised covert radio equipment, 14 Intelligence Company signallers were trained in very basic CQB drills with both pistols and small arms. The CQB training brought covert signallers up to a level of competence that far surpassed that of normal uniformed soldiers but their skills never reached the standard of regular Det operators. Signallers were also trained in rudimentary covert operational procedures to help them avoid detection when working in potentially hostile environments.

Each 14 Intelligence Company operator carried a personal encrypted radio when out on operations. An earpiece, hidden under the long hair the soldiers sported, enabled them to receive messages, while a concealed throat mike made it possible to give a running commentary while moving about on foot. Each car also had its own encrypted radio set and internal microphone, which allowed operators hands-free communications when mobile. To help them blend into the local area, operators often 'personalised' their cars, adding small touches such as shopping bags or children's cots in the rear seats so that they looked much the same as any other civilian vehicle.

All Dets carried out routine surveillance in republican areas on a day-to-day basis, both to familiarise themselves with the environment and to gather routine information on the movements of known 'faces'. However, major operations were almost always based on intelligence, which was provided to the unit by RUC Special Branch and MI5. To collate and sift the information they received and acquired, the Det had a number of specially recruited and trained Military Intelligence Liaison Officers (MLOs), who regularly attended briefings with MI5 and the RUC. Like the signals section of the unit, MLOs received advanced training at Pontrilas, both on their specialised role within 14 Intelligence Company and in CQB drills and basic covert procedures.

The MLOs sifted and graded the intel they received, then put it in a form that would be accessible and useful to the operators. They then briefed the relevant Det units, who would go on to mount targeted surveillance operations using the information. On rare occasions, the intelligence was 'real time', meaning that an attack was imminent. In such cases, 14 Intelligence Company would 'crash out' operators in an attempt to identify the terrorists and thwart the attack. More usually, though, the information had a longer shelf life and this made it possible to plan a deliberate and carefully orchestrated operation.

An early example of this sort of operation took place in June 1974. The Belfast Det received intelligence from an MLO working with Special Branch that loyalist terrorists were planning a major military offensive in North Belfast. An intensive surveillance operation was launched against known loyalist paramilitaries in order to discover who was involved and provide information to support the disruption of the planned attacks. The Det unit tracked several weapons as they were being moved to an Orange Order Hall on Belfast's Shankill Road. On 12 June, the local security force unit was tasked to search the building. Inside, they discovered an arsenal of weapons intended for use in the upcoming offensive. This intelligence-led surveillance operation prevented a significant escalation of the sectarian violence then plaguing the city.

Routine surveillance of known and suspected terrorist figures could also pay off in style. In August 1974, information gathered by the Belfast Det and collated by MLOs led to the arrest of 28 members of the PIRA. The men captured included the current Belfast Brigade commander, continuing the unlucky run for those who held that post.

The main function of 14 Intelligence Company was to gather intelligence rather than to directly engage terrorists. However, despite all the efforts made by operators to blend into the background, it was impossible to plan for every possible unexpected circumstance. On 20 January 1975, two operators from the Mid Ulster Det ran into a PIRA roadblock at Cassidy's Cross, near Kinawley in south-west Fermanagh. The roadblock was part of the Fermanagh Brigade's campaign to assert their authority in the area and make it ungovernable. When the operators stumbled across the unexpected roadblock, the PIRA terrorists were in the process of hijacking a bus. The operators felt they had no choice but to engage. There was a brief exchange of gunfire, during which PIRA Volunteer Kevin Coen was killed. Coen was a citizen of the Irish Republic who had joined the PIRA's Southern Command in 1971 and later came north to take the fight to the British.

The frequency with which republican paramilitaries hijacked vehicles was a constant danger to men who spent much of their time driving around republican strongholds. On 12 December 1977, an operator in the Londonderry Det was carrying out routine mobile surveillance duties when his car was approached by two men, Colm McNutt and Patrick Phelan, both Irish National Liberation Army (INLA) terrorists. McNutt told the operator to wind down his window and asked him what he was doing in the area. Falling back on his training, the operator replied in his best Belfast accent, 'I'm waiting for my girl.' This may have persuaded the INLA men that the operator was just a local resident but it did nothing to deter them from trying to steal his car. McNutt opened his jacket to reveal a revolver and informed the operator that he was taking the vehicle. Biding his time, the operator got out as ordered and waited while Phelan climbed into the driver's seat. Then, as McNutt walked around the car to the passenger side, the operator drew his Browning 9mm and double tapped the terrorist, dropping him with two rounds to the centre mass. Phelan scrambled from the car and fled. The operator got back into the now-vacant driver's seat and quickly drove away.

Colm McNutt died at the scene. Phelan was later arrested by the RUC and successfully prosecuted for the attempted hijacking of the Det car. Nine years later, after his release from prison, Patrick Phelan was killed in New York while drunk by an off-duty NYPD officer.

The shooting of McNutt led to accusations that he had been 'set up' by INLA informer Raymond Gilmore and that undercover soldiers were operating a 'shoot to kill' policy. Neither claim has any basis in reality. The operator who killed McNutt was simply on a routine surveillance operation and took the action he believed was appropriate to protect himself and his vehicle from an armed hijacking.

The legacy left by the regrettable actions of the MRF now resurfaced. The PIRA propaganda machine went into overdrive in an attempt to tie McNutt's killing to earlier actions and put them together as evidence that the British Army was operating plainclothes assassination squads in Ulster. These claims, while completely without merit, gained traction among many on the left wing of British politics, as well as in the United States, especially among those of Irish descent. Such accusations were to become one of the recurring features of the undercover war and were repeated again and again after almost every operation that ended in a terrorist death.

Two days after the Londonderry shooting, on 14 December 1977, Corporal Paul Harman of the Belfast Det was carrying out routine surveillance in the Turf Lodge area of Belfast. He was stopped at the junction of Monagh Road and Monagh

Avenue by a local PIRA unit attempting another carjacking. Corporal Harman exited the car and engaged his attackers. Unfortunately, possibly in response to McNutt's shooting, the PIRA team were covered by a concealed sniper and Corporal Harman was shot dead. His body was stripped of everything he was carrying, including his personal radio and weapon. The car was looted and burned.

The killing of Corporal Harman was a cruel blow to all 14 Intelligence Company operators, driving home to every member of the Det the danger they faced on even routine operations. It is not known whether the attack on a second Det car in such a short period of time was merely a coincidence or whether McNutt's killing had drawn the PIRA's attention to the mobile surveillance cars working in their areas. What we do know is that with Corporal Harman's murder, a PIRA unit had, for the first time, been afforded a detailed look at a Det surveillance vehicle, concealed radios, door holster and all. If their interest had not been aroused previously, now it was with a vengeance. In the days following Corporal Harman's killing, the Det heard from both Special Branch and MI5 sources that the PIRA had instructed its units to capture a surveillance operator alive for interrogation.

More than any other possible outcome, including being shot dead or blown up, the prospect of being captured by the PIRA sent a chill down the spine of every undercover soldier. Operators were given specific advice on what to do if caught: they were to talk and make themselves appear useful but without giving away any sensitive information. The goal was to keep themselves alive for as long as possible in order to give the security forces the best possible chance of rescuing them. Each operator was issued with a locator device and plans were put in place to seal off any area in which an operator had been captured. The area would then be swamped with security personnel tasked to conduct house-to-house searches until the missing man was found. In reality, the chances of being rescued were extremely slim. Every operator knew that the almost certain outcome of capture was a long, slow, painful period of torture, followed inevitably by death.

While the PIRA leadership continued to claim for propaganda purposes that undercover SAS teams were patrolling republican areas, they were now aware that a new opponent had entered the fray. They concluded that this previously unknown covert unit was responsible for the devastating setbacks the PIRA had suffered over the previous year. In response, the PIRA began to reorganise itself, moving away from a quasi-military structure based on brigades, battalions and companies, towards one more suited to covert warfare.

The new structure was based around independent cells or Active Service Units (ASUs). These units were locally led and highly compartmentalised. Contacts with other ASUs were minimised to ensure that if one unit was compromised, the British surveillance teams would not be able to follow an easy trail to other units. One of the first tasks of the reorganised ASUs was to actively target 14 Intelligence Company operators.

Both sides knew it was only a matter of time before there was another clash. When it came, it was not on the streets of Belfast but in a rural observation post in County Londonderry. In early March 1978, RUC Special Branch received intelligence that a particularly active and vicious PIRA hit team was using the Glenshane Pass area of Londonderry as a staging post for their attacks. The team was thought to include Dominic McGlinchey, Francis Hughes and Ian Milne, all known terrorists.

Initially, the SAS were tasked with setting up an OP on the Pass (the SAS were finally sent to Ulster in an official capacity in 1976, see Chapter Four). Knowing the potential opposition they faced, the SAS deployed a strong OP team consisting of four heavily-armed soldiers. The team staked out the area for several weeks but pressing operational priorities elsewhere meant they could not remain in place indefinitely. On 16 March 1978, the SAS handed over the OP to operators from 14 Intelligence Company.

While the SAS team had deployed with the possibility of combat in mind, the Londonderry Det's focus was solely on surveillance. For this reason, the four SAS troopers were replaced by just two Det operators. The night after the handover, at about 21.15, the operators spotted three armed men wearing camouflage clothing moving towards their position. The men in the OP were torn. While it was possible that these were the PIRA targets they had been tasked to find, the operators were also concerned that the approaching figures might be an Ulster Defence Regiment (UDR) patrol that had strayed into the area. Unwilling to open fire on fellow soldiers, one of the operators, Lance Corporal David

Jones, shouted a challenge. The terrorist ASU immediately opened fire in response.

In the firefight that followed, Lance Corporal Jones was killed and the other operator wounded. Before succumbing to his wounds, Lance Corporal Jones returned fire and wounded PIRA Volunteer Francis Hughes, who was captured in a nearby field the next morning. The other two PIRA men managed to escape. Hughes was later prosecuted for the murder of Lance Corporal Jones and sentenced to life imprisonment. He died in the Maze Prison in 1981 while undertaking a hunger strike.

Once again, the death of a Det member led to painful lessons being learned. The area around the Glenshane Pass OP had been placed out of bounds to all members of the security forces. Despite this, the operators had given away their position rather than risk a contact with friendly forces. Their scruples cost Lance Corporal Jones his life. Had the four-man SAS team still been in place, no warning would have been given beyond that required by the Yellow Card rules. The moment the PIRA terrorists raised their weapons they would have been killed. All of the Det's operators had the lesson driven home that in a close combat situation their only real assets were surprise and cover. Giving up either or both of these was a sure way to find yourself in a wooden box.

One of the more curious events in the undercover war occurred on the evening of 14 May 1977. Captain Robert Nairac, an MLO attached to 14 Intelligence Company, drove alone to the Three Steps pub in Dromintee, South Armagh. Later intelligence reports confirm that he told the regulars in the pub that his name was Danny McErlaine, a motor mechanic and member of the Official IRA from the Ardoyne area of North Belfast. The real McErlaine, on the run since 1974, was later killed by the PIRA in June 1978 after stealing arms from the organisation.

The same source reports that Captain Nairac got up and sang republican folksongs with the band playing that night. At around 11.45 p.m., Nairac was abducted by a group of men, most of whom were low-level members of the local PIRA. Following a fierce struggle in the pub's car park, Nairac was taken across the border into the Republic of Ireland, to a field in the Ravensdale Woods in County Louth. There, he was violently interrogated by his abductors. Despite the torture, Captain Nairac neither admitted his true identity nor revealed any information about 14 Intelligence Company operations. Terry McCormick, one of the men who took part in the abduction, went so far as to claim he was a priest in the hope that Nairac would give something away in his final confession. The only words he received in response were, 'Bless me, Father, for I have sinned.' Captain Nairac was shot dead by a PIRA gunman who had been summoned to the scene by the abductors.

Nairac was posthumously awarded the George Cross for gallantry. The citation states:

> Captain Nairac [...] was subjected to a succession of excep-tionally savage assaults in an attempt to extract information which would have put other lives and future operations at serious risk. These efforts to break Captain Nairac's will failed

entirely. Weakened as he was in strength – though not in spirit – by the brutality, he yet made repeated and spirited attempts to escape, but on each occasion was eventually overpowered by the weight of the numbers against him.

His body has never been found.

Claims that Captain Nairac was a member of the SAS or an operator with 14 Intelligence Company are completely untrue. His sole operational mandate was to liaise with Special Branch and MI5 and then brief Det operators on the intelligence he had received. However, he also had the reputation of a man who was willing to break the rules. An ex-UDR officer who accompanied Nairac on a drive reports being unexpectedly driven across the border into the Republic of Ireland to meet a contact. In an interview some 30 years later, he said, 'I told my ops officer Nairac was a loony and I wanted nothing more to do with him.'

What exactly Captain Nairac was doing in the Three Steps pub on 14 May 1977, nobody will ever really know. What is certain is that he was not there in an official capacity. Speculation in Special Forces circles, and it can only be speculation, is that Nairac was attempting to develop his own sources of intelligence, outside the official channels within which he was supposed to be working. His brutal death served as a savage reminder of the fate awaiting any undercover soldier who fell into the hands of the PIRA.

The hard lessons learned from the deaths of Corporal Harman in Belfast and Lance Corporal Jones on the Glenshane Pass were put to the test on 10 June 1978. That day, two PIRA volunteers made the mistake of trying to hijack a car driven by a pair of 14 Intelligence Company operators in Londonderry. Instead of playing along, as Harman had six months earlier, the operator in the passenger seat immediately opened fire. PIRA volunteer Dennis Heaney was shot with five bullets, killing him instantly. The other PIRA member fled, allowing the operators to escape the hostile area. An RUC search at the scene of the shooting recovered a weapon. Nevertheless, the IRA leadership claimed that Heaney had been gunned down in the street in cold blood. That night there was intense rioting in republican areas of Londonderry.

As a result of Heaney's death, the Derry Provisionals redoubled their counter-surveillance operations against the Londonderry Det. On 11 August 1978, one of their units spotted a Det operator, Lance Corporal Alan Swift, carrying out routine surveillance in the Brandywell area of the city. As the operator was driving down the Letterkenny Road, a hijacked Toyota van pulled up in front of him and at least two gunmen opened fire. Lance Corporal Swift had no chance to shoot back before he was killed.

From the time of its formation in 1973 up until the mid-1980s, 14 Intelligence Company had an operational strength, not including signallers and support staff, close to that of a normal infantry company. In such a small, tight-knit unit each operator was known, at least by sight, to every other man. The loss of an operator hit hard and was a personal affair for every Det member. The deaths of Corporal Harman and Lance Corporal Jones, while tragic, were seen by operators as part of the daily risks they faced when operating in hostile areas. The death of Lance Corporal Swift was something different. This was a targeted assassination, a directed and deliberate killing of a member of the unit. It was to have further tragic results.

The targeted murder of one of their own, coupled with the brutal killing of Captain Nairac, put every member of 14 Intelligence Company on edge. In September 1978, two members of the Mid Ulster Det were carrying out routine mobile operations near Lough Neagh. At the same time, James Taylor, a Protestant with no paramilitary affiliations, was out shooting pigeons with two friends in the same area.

When Taylor and his friends returned to their vehicle after the shoot, they discovered that someone had let the air out of the Land Rover's tyres in their absence. By freak chance, just as the repairs were being completed, the Det surveillance car happened to pass the scene. As they drove by, one of the operators inside burst out laughing at a joke made by his companion. Taylor and his friends, angry at the vandalism of their car, came to the conclusion that the laughing man was the responsible party. The three civilians jumped into their Land Rover and took off in pursuit.

The Det operators quickly became aware that they were being followed by a vehicle containing three roughly-dressed, hard-looking individuals. With recent events fresh in their minds, the operators suspected that they were being chased by a PIRA ASU. They pulled over to the side of the road, exited the car and prepared themselves for an immediate contact. The Land Rover came to a halt behind them and the three friends piled out, ready to confront the vandals. Taylor made the mistake of carrying his

shotgun with him when he left the vehicle. One of the Det operators was crouching behind the passenger-side door with a MAC-10
submachine gun in his hand resting on the seat inside. On seeing
the shotgun, he raised his weapon and fired, killing Taylor.

The republican press inevitably used the incident to repeat
their claims that undercover SAS assassination teams were
roaming the country and shooting men dead as part of their 'shoot
to kill' policy. The truth is that the Det operators honestly, and
not unreasonably, believed Taylor's party to be a PIRA hit team, a
view that appeared to be confirmed when Taylor approached them
carrying a weapon. They did nothing more than act in accordance
with their operational drills. In the bitter no-holds-barred covert
war that was being fought at the time, it is a testimony to the
discipline and training of all operators that such mistakes were
exceptionally rare.

As the decade came to a close, both sides took stock of their
respective positions. By the end of the 1970s, the Provisional IRA
knew that the complete military victory they had once hoped for
was not possible. Attempts to create 'no-go' zones for the security
forces in major urban centres had been rolled back and the PIRA
had been forced to abandon its quasi-military structure in favour
of small units carrying out independent operations. Planning
turned instead to the pursuit of a 'long war' strategy, in the belief
that a prolonged terrorist campaign would weaken British resolve
to stay in the province. To pursue this long war, the PIRA would
need new money, weapons and a strategy to deal with the threat
posed by British undercover units.

The PIRA drew their income from a number of different sources, ranging from protection rackets and bank robberies across Ireland, to donations from wealthy backers, especially among Irish-Americans in the USA. The bulk of the organisation's weapons were initially smuggled in from the United States, but they increasingly came to rely on huge arms shipments from Colonel Gaddafi's Libya. Ultimately, it was these weapons that would sustain the PIRA military machine right up until the end of the conflict.

In an attempt to combat the increasing penetration of their organisation by both MI5 and RUC Special Branch, the PIRA formed internal security units whose sole function was to seek out and eliminate suspected informers. Anyone suspected of providing information to the British was subject to torture and summary execution. It is an ironic twist of fate that the senior member of the PIRA responsible for internal security was, in fact, an MI5 double agent.

The Provisional IRA, as well as other republican terrorist organisations, also began to train their members in basic anti-surveillance tactics. Lookouts, or 'dickers', were routinely deployed to try to spot surveillance teams. Before operations were mounted, ASUs would also frequently carry out dummy runs in the hope of drawing into the open any covert units who were watching them or their targets.

On the British side, by the end of 1979, the overall command and control of undercover units had undergone a radical reorganisation (see Chapter Six). A consequence of this was that

14 Intelligence Company began both to receive better intelligence and to work more closely with the SAS and other undercover units. As a result, the British Army's undercover war was to become much better coordinated and, unfortunately for the PIRA volunteers in the field, much more deadly efficient.

CHAPTER FOUR

A SAVAGE WAR

THE SECOND DEPLOYMENT OF THE SAS (1974–79)

On 10 February 1975, the Provisional IRA and the British government entered into a ceasefire. The general terms of the truce were that the PIRA would stop their attacks on the British security forces and the security forces would, in turn, curtail their searches and raids in republican areas. The ceasefire agreement was a matter of considerable controversy within the republican organisation. Some hardline elements, especially in the border units of South Armagh and Tyrone, wanted no part in any cessation of violence. These units were dedicated advocates of the 'physical force' doctrine who believed that an outright military victory over the 'Brits' was not only possible but inevitable.

The border units either saw the truce as little more than a pause in the military campaign or they ignored it completely. The following are just a few of the attacks that took place during the supposed 'ceasefire'.

- 7 July 1975 – RUC officer killed by a booby-trap bomb planted by the PIRA's North Armagh Brigade at a school in Lurgan, County Armagh.

- 17 July 1975 – South Armagh Brigade kills four British soldiers in a remote-controlled bomb attack near Forkhill, County Armagh.

- 22 November 1975 – three British soldiers shot dead by South Armagh PIRA in a gun attack on an observation post near Crossmaglen, County Armagh.

- 25 November 1975 – two RUC officers shot dead on patrol by members of North Armagh PIRA.

The 'truce' also did little to interrupt a vicious shooting and bombing campaign being carried out in mainland Britain by an Active Service Unit that came to be known as the Balcombe Street Gang. Over a period of a year and a half, the Balcombe Street Gang ASU executed dozens of bombing and shooting attacks in London, killing 19 people. On 6 December 1975, four members of the unit – Martin O'Connell, Edward Butler, Harry Duggan and Hugh Doherty – were chased and cornered by Metropolitan Police officers after carrying out a drive-by shooting on a restaurant. The terrorists fled into a flat on Balcombe Street, where they took hostages and demanded a plane to fly them to the Republic of Ireland. The SAS anti-terrorist team was called in by the Home

Office in order to end the siege. On 12 December, screens were erected around the building in preparation for an assault. The PIRA unit, sensing what was coming, released their hostages and surrendered. The killers were arrested, tried and given sentences totalling 600 years.

Faced with an unrelenting and vicious terrorist campaign in both Ulster and the mainland, the British military saw the truce as a misguided project. Indeed, some even saw it as a deliberate attempt by politicians to hinder their efforts to tackle terrorism in the province. Most ordinary soldiers believed that they were already operating with one hand tied behind their back; during the 'truce', they felt that the other hand was bound up as well.

As far as the undercover war was concerned, the ceasefire had little effect on the activities of MI5 and RUC Special Branch, and both services used the period to intensify their efforts to infiltrate the PIRA and INLA. Meanwhile, 14 Intelligence Company was busier than ever, with the number of surveillance operations carried out against republican and loyalist terrorists more than doubling.

Apart from the continuing activity of the PIRA border units, the main reason for the increase in 14 Intelligence Company's operations was the spectacular rise in sectarian violence and killings that took place during the 'truce'. Loyalist paramilitaries believed that the ceasefire was a sign of weakness and feared a softening of British resolve to remain in Ulster. They responded by increasing their attacks on the Catholic population in the province in the hope of forcing the PIRA into retaliation, thus ending the truce or even provoking an outright civil war.

In 1975 alone, loyalist terrorists killed 120 Catholics, the vast majority of them innocent civilians. The PIRA, INLA and some rogue elements of the Official IRA (which itself maintained a separate truce with the British Army) eagerly took up the loyalist challenge and a brutal wave of tit-for-tat killings began to spiral out of control. The increasing violence came to a savage head when, on 4 January 1976, loyalists shot dead six Catholic civilians in two coordinated attacks in South Armagh. Three members of the Reavey family were slaughtered at their home in Whitecross and three members of the O'Dowd family at their home in Ballydougan.

Late in the afternoon of 5 January 1976, shortly after 5.30 p.m., PIRA men operating under the cover name of the South Armagh Republican Action Force responded by carrying out one of the most infamous sectarian killings of the Troubles. A minibus carrying twelve workers home from their jobs in a textile factory was flagged down near the village of Kingsmill by a man wearing a military-style combat uniform. The occupants initially believed they had run into a British Army checkpoint. However, as the vehicle came to a halt, eleven more armed men in uniform broke cover and surrounded the bus.

One of the gunmen pulled the door open and demanded to know who among the occupants was a Catholic. Richard Hughes, the lone Catholic among the otherwise Protestant workers, was ordered to leave and the remaining men were removed from the vehicle and lined up outside. The gunmen then opened fire in what can only be described as a cold-blooded orgy of violence. The eleven Protestants were mown down at close range with a variety of automatic weapons. In all, at least 136 rounds were fired. According to some reports, one of the gunmen then moved among the bodies to finish each man off with a pistol shot to the head. Only one of the textile workers, Alan Black, survived, despite being shot 18 times.

The Kingsmill massacre caused outrage, not just in the province of Ulster but throughout Britain. There were repeated calls for the government of the day to 'do something' to stop the slaughter of innocents along the border, and specifically in South Armagh. The government responded by declaring County Armagh a 'Special Emergency Area' and deploying hundreds of extra troops and police. A few weeks after the massacre, the government announced that the SAS was being sent into South Armagh.

Unlike the first deployment of the regiment, this second deployment was an emergency situation and it was only possible to send a single reinforced troop. The Troop (as the SAS presence in Northern Ireland came to be known in undercover circles, whatever its actual establishment might be at a given time) took up residence in a secure compound in a military barracks in the largely Protestant town of Portadown. From there, they began to insert plainclothes patrols and two-man covert observation posts at critical points along the border.

The unit that was sent to the province had no time for any build-up training. Most of the men deployed were combat veterans who had recently completed a tour in Dhofar, the same small undeclared war from which B Squadron had returned before their unofficial tour several years before. Many had never served in the province before and had little understanding of the political complexities of the situation and the limitations placed on soldiers serving there.

This was shown clearly in one of the first briefings given by a patrol commander tasked with setting up an ambush close to the border. The corporal in charge of the operation was a legendary and highly decorated Fijian soldier. The Regimental Sergeant Major (RSM) was present to oversee matters and to make sure that operational planning fell in line with the political requirements in force in Ulster. According to SAS legend, the briefing was rife with confusion.

'Right, lads,' the corporal announced, turning to a map of the operational area on which he pointed out key locations, 'we'll be dropped off here and then we'll make our way across to the ambush position here. The terrorists will approach from that direction, and when they reach this location, I'll shoot them.'

At this point, the RSM interrupted, shaking his head: 'No ... you can't shoot them.'

The Fijian NCO paused for a few moments to collect his thoughts. 'Right, right, understood.' He turned back to his men and pointed towards another member of the team. 'OK, when they reach this location, *you* shoot them.'

The RSM interrupted again, an exasperated look on his face now. 'No! Look, you're not understanding me. You have to *grab* them.'

The Fijian NCO paused again to think, then nodded in recognition as he suddenly saw the wisdom of the RSM's words.

'Got it, got it.' Turning back to the patrol, he explained the revised plan: 'Right, lads, when they reach this location, *I'll* grab them then *you* shoot them.'

Ironically, just as the Troop were grappling with the limitations of their new role, the PIRA units in South Armagh believed that the SAS had been given *carte blanche* to eliminate them by any means necessary. This fear was heightened when, on 15 April 1976, an SAS team captured a top PIRA killer by the name of Peter Cleary. Cleary had been on the run in the Republic of Ireland for two weeks following his suspected involvement in the killing of UDR Corporal Robert McConnell. When he slipped back across the border to see his pregnant girlfriend near Forkhill, an SAS team that had spent a week watching her house moved in and arrested him.

Since road travel was considered too dangerous because of the ever-present threat of landmines, Cleary was taken to a nearby field to be picked up by a military helicopter. As the four-man SAS team were attempting to guide the helicopter in to land, Cleary took advantage of their distraction and tried to grab a rifle from one of his guards. He was shot dead in the attempt. Cleary was the first person killed by the SAS in Northern Ireland. His death sent a shockwave through the South Armagh PIRA. Many senior members of the unit, believing Cleary had been executed and that the SAS intended to kill them all in cold blood, retreated across the border.

SAS activities increased in intensity over the following months. However, the lack of local knowledge and the absence of any proper build-up training resulted in some of these early operations ending in farce.

On 2 May 1976, Seamus Ludlow was kidnapped and murdered near Dundalk in the Republic of Ireland. To this day his murder remains unsolved but many believed at the time, and continue to believe, that loyalist paramilitaries crossed the border to carry out the killing. As a direct result of these suspicions, the Republic's security forces stepped up their presence along the South Armagh border in an attempt to interdict any further incursions. As part of this effort, the Gardaí, supported by a contingent from the Irish Army, set up a security checkpoint on Flagstaff Road, a short distance inside the Republic.

At 10.40 p.m. on 5 May, a Triumph 200 with two men inside approached the checkpoint from the north. The Gardaí officers flagged the vehicle down and asked the occupants, one of whom was, to their surprise, Fijian, where they were going. The suspicions of the officers were further aroused when the pair were unable to give a satisfactory answer to the simple question. The men were forced out of the car at gunpoint and the vehicle was searched. Inside were two firearms, a Sterling submachine gun and a 9mm Browning pistol. The men, both members of the recently deployed SAS troop, were immediately arrested and taken to a nearby Garda station.

At 2.05 in the morning, a car carrying another four SAS men drove into the same checkpoint, completely unaware of what had happened to their colleagues a few hours earlier. Moments later, a second vehicle delivered two more members of the Troop straight into the arms of the bewildered Gardaí officers. Despite pleas to be allowed to return across the border, the six men were disarmed and taken to Dundalk police station. All eight SAS men were charged with illegal possession of firearms, pleaded guilty and were fined.

The incident was a major embarrassment for the SAS and a propaganda bonanza for the PIRA. Here, they claimed, was proof positive that the SAS were carrying out armed operations south of the Irish border, where they were engaged in the assassination of Irish citizens. The debacle also caused a major diplomatic rift between the British and Irish governments.

The true cause of the incident was error rather than malice. A two-man SAS covert observation post had been inserted just north of the border as part of the ongoing operation to identify and interdict PIRA movements from the Republic. The first pair of soldiers the Gardaí arrested were on their way to relieve the OP. Unfortunately, imprecise maps and faulty navigation led them to stray across the border. When the relieving troops failed to turn up at the appointed time, the men in the OP sent an emergency signal back to base. Fearing the first car had been ambushed, two more vehicles were sent out to retrieve the soldiers in the OP and then locate the two missing men. However, once the observation team had been picked up, the two cars then made exactly the same mistake as the men they were looking for and ran into the same checkpoint. The operation ended up making the SAS look more like the Keystone Kops than highly professional soldiers. In order to ensure that similar mistakes were never made again, the

SAS put in place a comprehensive programme of build-up training for the next troop deployed to the province.

Despite the cross-border debacle, the deployment of the SAS to South Armagh led to a significant reduction in PIRA activity over the next five months, as was pointed out by Ulster Unionist MP James McCusker on the floor of the House of Commons:

> A lot has been said about the introduction of the Special Air Service into South Armagh. I know that its introduction was considered unacceptable by many people for a long time. I do not want to tempt fate, and I do not doubt for a minute that the IRA could be guilty of a terrible atrocity in South Armagh this very night. There is no point in keeping our fingers crossed and closing our eyes to the possibility. But the point is that for five months in South Armagh, since the SAS went in, we have had a degree of civilisation, much more so than we have had there for a long time. There may be an incident tonight or tomorrow that will change the situation immediately, but even this will not change the fact that the introduction of the SAS has made a difference.*

The 1970s saw an unprecedented wave of terrorist attacks throughout the Western world. Left- and right-wing political extremists took up arms in Germany, France, Italy, Spain and the US. Planes and boats were hijacked on an almost-monthly basis; Basque and

---

* Hansard, 14 June 1976, Volume 913.

Irish terrorists carried out shootings and bombings to further their nationalist agendas; and the Arab-Israeli conflict bubbled over onto European shores with shocking acts of violence such as the massacre of Olympic athletes in Munich. In order to ensure that the UK had a specialist force able to respond to such incidents, the SAS committed one of their four squadrons on a rotating basis as a dedicated anti-terrorist team. The assigned squadron fielded two complete teams, Red and Blue, who trained exclusively to deal with plane hijacking and urban terrorism incidents in mainland Britain. This squadron also acted as an immediate reserve if additional personnel were required for any other major SAS operations.

The SAS troop deployed to operate in Ulster was detached from the squadron serving in the anti-terrorist team rotation. In order to rectify the shortcomings that had blighted the first SAS deployment in 1976, when the next squadron began its training to take over the anti-terrorist role, the troop destined for Northern Ireland followed a specialised programme of its own. This better prepared them for the nature of operations in the province, as the next encounter with the South Armagh PIRA was to show.

In early January 1977, a suspect car was discovered concealed in dense woodland by a metalled road near Crossmaglen, South Armagh. A four-man SAS team from G Squadron was tasked to stake out the area in the hope of discovering who had concealed it and why. On 16 January, after more than a week of waiting, the team's patience paid off when the men in the OP heard the sounds of a vehicle approaching. They listened as the vehicle came to a halt nearby but out of sight. A door was heard to open and a few moments later, a masked man appeared, moving towards the suspect car with a pump-action shotgun in his hands.

The team burst into action: two members of the patrol split off and made their way quickly through the woods in the direction of the unseen vehicle; the remaining pair, meanwhile, broke cover and rushed forward to intercept the armed man. As he caught sight of them, the terrorist turned and swung his weapon round to engage. Both soldiers opened fire, instantly killing the man.

The other two SAS men dashed towards the metalled road, where they could hear the second vehicle driving away. Once they reached the edge of the road, they paused, unwilling to give up the cover of the trees before they could ascertain the situation. It was the right decision. The van was rolling slowly away with its back doors open. As soon as the soldiers came into sight, two gunmen inside opened fire with a hail of rounds from their automatic weapons. Fortunately, neither SAS man was hit.

The dead terrorist was Seamus Harvey, a member of the South Armagh PIRA. The empty cases found at the scene, from an Armalite and a Garand rifle, were forensically tested by the RUC and directly linked to the weapons used in the Kingsmill massacre. RUC Special Branch and MI5 had little doubt that Harvey himself was one of the men involved in the atrocity.

The success of this operation was a major blow to the local PIRA. It also restored some of the confidence in the SAS that had been lost in the missteps of late 1976, convincing both the

Army's High Command and the security services more broadly of the regiment's effectiveness. As a result, SAS operations were expanded to other areas of the province. The new trust in the unit soon paid off. On 26 February 1978, two members of the PIRA's East Tyrone Brigade were ambushed by a concealed SAS team as they attempted to retrieve explosives from a derelict house near Washing Bay. Paul Duffy was killed and another PIRA volunteer wounded as he escaped in a car.

Any satisfaction felt by the SAS as a result of these successes was tempered by the death of Staff Sergeant Dave Naden in a car accident. He was a well-liked and highly respected member of the regiment and was the first member of the SAS to die on operations in Ulster.

In June 1978, the SAS were deployed to Belfast for the first time, acting on source intelligence provided by RUC Special Branch. This intelligence came from a highly placed informer in the PIRA's 3rd Battalion, based in the Ardoyne area in the north of the city. The information passed on to the SAS team was that a four-man PIRA ASU intended to attack the Ballysillan post office using explosive incendiary devices. According to the source, at least one member of the ASU would be armed with a handgun.

Just after midnight on 21 June, the ASU arrived at the post office, where they were ambushed by the SAS team while unloading the explosive devices. Three of the men were killed almost instantly: PIRA Volunteers Jackie Mailey, Denis Brown and James Mulvenna. A fourth man also died: William Hanna, a Protestant, was mistaken for the final member of the ASU and shot by the SAS in a nearby field as he walked home. The actual fourth PIRA man made a frantic escape from the scene on foot. At a nearby roadblock, an RUC unit opened fire on a car and wounded another innocent civilian.

Within Special Branch and military intelligence, the Ballysillan ambush was seen as a major success, a hammer blow to the Ardoyne PIRA, which had been particularly active in recent months. This view was not shared by the upper echelons of the RUC. In particular, the then Deputy Chief Constable John Harmon believed that the death of an innocent civilian could not be balanced out by the destruction of a PIRA unit.

There was now an open disagreement between Special Branch in Belfast, supported by MI5, who wanted more such SAS operations in the city, and the RUC command, who clearly viewed the Ballysillan incident as an example of military 'overkill'. Senior RUC officers stated openly that they did not want gun battles between the SAS and PIRA on the streets of Belfast. The RUC command won the day and the SAS was not tasked to operate in the capital of the province again for several years.

Barely a month after the Ballysillan shootings, in early July 1978, the SAS became embroiled in one of the most unfortunate shootings of the entire undercover war. The tragic sequence of events began when John Boyle, the 16-year-old son of a local farmer, discovered a concealed arms cache in a graveyard. The cache contained an Armalite rifle, a pistol and other terrorist materials. The boy informed his father, Con Boyle, who in turn passed the information on to the RUC.

A four-man SAS team was deployed in a covert OP to watch the location. Apparently driven by curiosity about his earlier find, John Boyle returned to the graveyard on 11 July to have another look at his discovery. As he examined the weapons, John was shot dead by two members of the OP team. John's father heard the gunfire and rushed to the graveyard with his other son, Harry, where they were detained until the RUC arrived.

The RUC quickly discovered that the victim was an innocent, a boy who found himself in the wrong place at the wrong time. The already tense situation was then inflamed further by conflicting accounts of the shooting, given first by the two SAS men at the scene and then, later, in statements released by the Army Press Office in Lisburn. The press, unsurprisingly, had a field day pointing out the many inconsistencies in the differing stories given by the military. The fact that the Armalite John had allegedly picked up was unloaded, contradicting the Army's initial claims that it had a magazine fitted and a round in the breech, caused particular outrage among some commentators.

To say that the RUC was upset by the shooting would be a gross understatement. Many of its officers were incandescent with rage and openly challenged the Army's version of events. The clamour for a prosecution of the men involved in the incident became unanswerable and eventually the Army yielded to the inevitable. Corporal Alan Bohan and Trooper Ron Temperley of the SAS were officially charged with the murder of John Boyle.

The men were brought to trial under Northern Ireland's Diplock court system, which allowed charges relating to the

Troubles to be decided by a judge in the absence of a jury. This most serious of cases was presided over by the head of the Northern Ireland judiciary, Lord Chief Justice Sir Robert Lowry.* Both of the defendants gave evidence before the court and the judge also heard from forensics experts. Despite being openly critical of the evidence given by the SAS men, and despite describing Corporal Bohan as an 'untrustworthy witness', Lord Lowry acquitted both men of murder. He could not, he set out in his judgment, state beyond a reasonable doubt that the soldiers were guilty. While their testimony was unreliable, he said, it remained possible that John Boyle had pointed a weapon in their direction, and this would have been enough to make the shooting legal. Corporal Bohan and Trooper Temperley were the only members of the SAS to stand trial for murder in the course of the undercover war.

In September 1978, a highly placed informer inside the PIRA's Derry Brigade informed his Special Branch handler of the presence of an arms dump in an unoccupied house. The hide contained bomb-making equipment as well as a number of rifles. The Londonderry Det carried out a covert search of the building and confirmed that the weapons were located in a wardrobe on the first floor.

An SAS team was deployed to watch the cache. Two men took up positions inside the house, in a bedroom away from the wardrobe. Another pair covered the front of the house from a nearby

---

* Lowry was created a life peer the following year.

building. At approximately 21.20 on 24 November, John Duffy, a quartermaster with the Derry PIRA, entered the house and made his way to the concealed arms. As he was examining the weapons, the two SAS men emerged from the nearby bedroom and challenged him. Duffy was shot dead as he spun around holding a weapon. Both soldiers later received a Mention in Dispatches for their role in the shooting.

The shootings by the SAS in Ballysillan, Dunloy and Londonderry (as well as the shooting of James Taylor by the Mid Ulster Det near Coagh) led to increasingly loud claims that the SAS were operating a 'shoot to kill' policy in the province. These allegations, given substance by the regrettable actions of the MRF, are one of the great republican fictions of the Troubles. It is certainly true that, unlike the police who frequently shot to disable, whenever an SAS member or Det operator opened fire, he did intend to kill his target. But the republican propaganda machine leveraged this undisputed fact to make a very different claim. They argued that SAS teams were briefed to kill and that when they went out on an operation, they did so with the explicit goal of killing any terrorists they encountered.

There is no truth whatsoever to these claims. No undercover soldier, either in the Det or the SAS, was ever specifically told to kill a suspected terrorist. On the contrary, it was made perfectly clear to all involved that if they opened fire, they would have to justify their actions under the 'Yellow Card' rules of engagement. Still, a reader may be tempted to think that the frequency with which terrorists were shot as they turned in reaction to a challenge, or as they began to raise a weapon, is rather suspicious. But this was simply a consequence of operational conditions.

In order to detain and charge a suspect, it was not enough for them simply to be in the vicinity of a weapons cache. For charges to stick in court, the target of the operation actually had to be in possession of an illegal weapon. This requirement meant waiting until the suspect had picked up a firearm before moving in. Once the suspect was armed, though, the range of possible outcomes narrowed dramatically. The Det and the SAS both knew that in the PIRA and the INLA they faced ruthless, highly motivated terrorists who would not hesitate to kill. The hard lessons learned from the deaths of Captain Pollen in 1974 and Lance Corporal Jones in 1978 showed that giving an armed terrorist the chance to open fire in a close-combat situation would often result in the death of a soldier. Under such circumstances, it is hardly surprising that Special Forces operators took few risks. Unless the suspect immediately stopped moving and dropped their weapon when challenged, the logic of the situation often drove those involved inexorably towards a fatal outcome. An armed man can turn and bring a weapon to bear in a fraction of a second, so any physical motion that could possibly have ended with a gun barrel pointing towards a soldier was liable to be interpreted as a genuine threat. And the appropriate response to such a threat was to remove it as quickly and conclusively as possible. The SAS encapsulated the attitude of all undercover soldiers in a simple saying: 'It's better to be judged by twelve than carried by six.'

Some will say that this is unfair, that when surprised and challenged, it is entirely natural for a person to turn towards the source of the noise. That may well be true. However, it is unreasonable to place the burden of risk in such a situation on a soldier carrying out his lawful duty. The moment of danger arises from the decision of the terrorist to arm himself and pursue his ends outside the law through acts of violence. The difficult and dangerous position he finds himself in when challenged is nobody's responsibility but his own.

As the 1970s drew to a close, those in charge of the undercover war took stock of SAS operations in Ulster. On the one hand, there had been major successes. Since the initial insertion of the SAS into South Armagh, the unit had killed seven PIRA terrorists and been instrumental in the capture of many more. On the other hand, two innocent civilians had also died and the regiment had been embarrassed over the arrest of eight men by the Gardaí and the murder trial of two of its soldiers.

Taken as a whole, the Army and the RUC believed that the SAS had proved itself to be a vital cutting edge against the unremitting terrorist campaign ongoing in the province. However, there was much that could still be done to improve the way that edge was applied. Within the intelligence community, plans were being drawn up to better coordinate the various undercover units working in Northern Ireland in an effort to disrupt and degrade both the PIRA and the INLA. The SAS was seen as having a critical role to play in the campaign to come.

As part of this major reorganisation, a number of changes were made. The SAS moved their base of operations from Portadown to a secure and well-connected location on the Belfast side of Lough Neagh. This new location allowed the Troop to operate easily across the whole of the province. If the order came to 'crash out', cars could be in central Belfast in 25 minutes and in Londonderry or South Armagh in an hour.

A further important development came in the wake of the Dunloy shooting and the chaos of conflicting reports that had followed. A new system of strict post-contact procedures, called 'Ultra Marine', was instituted. After any shooting in which under-cover soldiers took part, the men involved were to be removed quickly from the area and taken to a secure location. Here, they would be debriefed and witness statements prepared by a specialist team of military lawyers. Only then would the men involved be passed on to the RUC for further interviews.

On 27 August 1979, the PIRA's South Armagh Brigade ambushed a convoy of vehicles from the 2nd Battalion of the Parachute Regiment, exploding two large roadside bombs at Narrow Water Castle, near the town of Warrenpoint. The first bomb was aimed at the convoy itself, while the second targeted the reinforcements sent to deal with the incident. IRA volunteers hidden in nearby woodland also allegedly fired on the troops. Eighteen paratroopers were killed and six were seriously injured. An English civilian was also killed and another injured when paratroopers fired across the border at suspected gunmen. On the same fateful day, the IRA assassinated Earl Louis Mountbatten, destroying his fishing boat with a bomb that also killed three others, including two children.

In the wake of these events, the SAS troop that was about to be deployed to the province were briefed that their coming operations would be increased in scope, scale and territorial range. The troop believed that the government, in direct response to the atrocities of 27 August, intended to give the SAS licence to cross the Irish border and attack known PIRA training camps in the Republic. They began to train for such an eventuality. Whether this course of action was, in fact, actively considered by the recently elected Conservative government cannot be established. If it was, saner heads eventually prevailed and the SAS was never given the authority to conduct cross-border operations. Nevertheless, with the major reorganisation of all covert operations, the undercover war was about to enter a new phase. Over the coming years, the PIRA would find itself under a kind of pressure it had never felt before.

CHAPTER FIVE

RE-ORGANISATION

THE RUC ENTERS THE FRAY

In the aftermath of the Warrenpoint massacre and the killing of Earl Mountbatten, a major review of all covert operating procedures in the province was carried out by a senior member of MI6. This systematic study resulted in one of the most crucial innovations of the undercover war, the formation of the Tasking and Co-ordination Groups (TCGs). The first TCG was set up in Castlereagh in Belfast in late 1979, closely followed by another at Gough Barracks in Armagh the same year. In 1980, a third unit was added, this time in Londonderry. The intended role of the TCGs was to control all undercover operations in their assigned areas. Belfast TCG managed operations in the capital of the province, South TCG covered Mid Ulster and South Armagh, while North TCG was responsible for the city of Londonderry and County Londonderry.

With the introduction of the TCGs, all relevant units were, for the first time, overseen by a single coordinating command structure. At the core of the TCGs were liaison officers drawn from the Army and the RUC, all of whom had operational experience in the field. They were supported in their work by additional liaison officers detached from MI5 and MI6. Together, this network of professional coordinators ensured that the free flow of information could fuel the next phase of the war.

The formation of the TCGs eliminated the inefficient duplication of work by the various Army and RUC undercover units. Instead of the *ad hoc* system that had previously been used to task individual teams for operations, all covert units could now be controlled centrally. This brought together under one roof the full range of British undercover capabilities and allowed careful coordination of operations with the regular Army and RUC units stationed in each region. With the new TCGs in control, proper out-of-bounds areas could now be created when operations were launched.

In order to strengthen collaborations with local units, a liaison officer from the SAS Troop in country was temporarily seconded to whichever Army unit had immediate responsibility for an operational area. The internal culture of the SAS being what it was, this role was usually assigned to the newest and least experienced member of the Troop. This arrangement sometimes caused difficulties, since the junior SAS man was given the nominal rank of Sergeant and lodged in the Sergeants' Mess for the duration of the operation.

In early 1981, a Trooper who had recently passed selection and joined the regiment from 2 Para was sent as a liaison to the unit he had left just a year before as a Private. When the newly minted Acting Sergeant walked into the mess, there was an uproar. This overturning of the natural order was felt by many to threaten the integrity of the military hierarchy, not to mention the dignity of the unit's long-service senior NCOs. 2 Para insisted that the man be replaced by a more senior member of the Troop. The traditionalists got their way and an existential crisis was averted.

The fixed mindsets common in military cultures worldwide sometimes clashed with the modern ethos of the TCGs in other ways. One frequent problem was that regular Army units were often eager for legitimate action to offset the tedious and dispiriting business of highly-constrained patrols in civilian areas. When they learned that an area was out of bounds due to an upcoming covert operation, it was not uncommon for unit commanders to set up vehicle checkpoints (VCPs) on the periphery in the hope of getting in on any action. This sort of reckless behaviour could threaten the success of an operation by deterring suspects from travelling to the target location. It could also have less predictable consequences.

In early 1981, a two-man SAS patrol wearing civilian clothes and driving an unmarked car withdrew from a covert OP in South Armagh. As they drove back towards their base in the pouring rain, they rounded a bend to find the road ahead blocked by a group of hooded armed men. Thinking they were still inside the out-of-bounds area, the SAS men believed they had run into a PIRA roadblock. They immediately halted their vehicle and spilled out of the doors carrying their Armalite rifles, ready to respond to the danger.

The roadblock was, in fact, a regular Army VCP manned by soldiers from the local unit, the hoods of their waterproof jackets pulled up to protect them from the driving rain. On seeing two armed men exit a car some distance from the checkpoint, they came to their own conclusion that they were being attacked by a PIRA ASU and immediately opened fire. Fortunately, the initial salvo missed the SAS men, who ducked into cover behind their car. Tragedy was averted when the pair heard Scottish voices calling to each other as the unit from the VCP advanced on the vehicle. One of the SAS men shouted out to the approaching soldiers, informing them that they were friendly, and a further exchange of fire was averted.

Despite the occasional difficulties stemming from units honouring the word but not the spirit of the out-of-bounds rules, the new procedures were, on the whole, a great success. The use of this new system by the TCGs all but eliminated the risk of friendly-fire incidents during covert operations in the province. Other organisational innovations were just as valuable. With a single, centralised command structure for each region, it was now possible to concentrate the products of intelligence-gathering operations in one place. Information flowed into the TCGs from a great variety of sources: surveillance reports from undercover units; patrol reports from uniformed soldiers on the street; technical sources, such as wiretaps on phones and MI5 listening devices in homes or offices; CCTV cameras; and, most importantly, informers within the terrorist organisations. All of this could now be collated, checked, evaluated and graded in a far more efficient manner.

The development of an operation would typically start with a source passing information on to his handler. This might be a report that a specific ASU intended to assassinate an off-duty member of the security forces. The intelligence would be passed by the handler to the relevant regional TCG for evaluation. The TCG then tasked either an RUC or Army surveillance unit to observe the ASU. Operators would hit the streets and follow known members of the unit to build up a more detailed picture of the individuals involved, their means of transport, locations of safe houses and the positions of arms caches. Once the surveillance unit had gathered enough intelligence and concluded that an attack was imminent, either the SAS or the RUC would be briefed to intercept and neutralise the targets.

Despite the professionalism of the TCGs and the enhanced collaboration they fostered, the new system did not completely eliminate inter-unit rivalries. This was especially true when it came to the difficult issue of informers. Sources inside terrorist organisations were a highly-prized and indispensable asset in the covert war but their cultivation was often a complex affair. Individual units could be extremely territorial when it came to their sources, both out of real concern for the safety of informers and because of the prestige gained by producing valuable intelligence.

Terrorists became 'sources' for a range of different reasons. Some, such as RUC source Eamon Collins and Gardaí source Sean O'Callaghan, turned on their former comrades as a matter of principle. These men, who had joined the PIRA out of a righteous indignation at the treatment of Catholics in the province, eventually came to see the PIRA for what it really was: a callous and murderous terrorist organisation needlessly escalating the violence that blighted Ulster. After a genuine change of heart, these brave individuals took enormous personal risks in order to protect lives and help bring the conflict to an end.

Other sources were motivated by less noble goals. For some, it was simply a question of self-enrichment. Being put on the payroll of the RUC or military intelligence appealed to more than a few men from impoverished backgrounds whose enthusiasm for the cause had waned as they left their youth behind. Others were blackmailed into becoming informers. A frequent lever exploited by the security services was sexual misconduct. As part of the PIRA's programme to maintain morale among the increasingly large number of imprisoned volunteers, harsh punishments were meted out to those who engaged in affairs with prisoners' wives. If a serving PIRA member was caught having sexual relations with a prisoner's wife, the inevitable result was knee-capping or sometimes even death. Faced with such extreme consequences, it is hardly surprising that many men became informers when confronted with photographic evidence of their transgressions.

Every source, regardless of their motivations for turning, had his own individual handler. RUC handlers were supervised by Special Branch while military sources came under the overall control of a branch of the Intelligence Corp called the Force Research Unit (FRU). Despite the efforts of the TCGs to promote inter-service harmony, a strong degree of competition remained between Special Branch and the various Army intelligence units.

In addition to the institutional prestige involved, a good source could make the career of the handler responsible for recruiting or running him.

This sibling rivalry among the services led indirectly to one of the biggest setbacks suffered by the British during the covert war. In 1994, following an attempt by Army handlers to 'poach' RUC informers, a special conference was called to settle the dispute. On the way to the meeting, a Chinook helicopter carrying 10 senior RUC officers, 9 Army intelligence officers and 6 MI5 officers crashed into a hillside on the Mull of Kintyre in Scotland. There were no survivors. The concentration of expertise lost in the accident was unparalleled in the whole of the Troubles.

Agent handlers in both the RUC and the Army were specially recruited and trained for their role. They often formed deep personal relations with their sources and protected them with all the ferocity of a she-wolf guarding her cubs. The response of the terrorist organisations to the discovery of an informer in their ranks was invariably the horrible torture and death of the man involved. When a handler lost a source, the personal impact was profound. In the early 1970s, a military intelligence handler committed suicide in Flax Street Mill, shooting himself in the head while in an OP. The handler had been brought to this point of despair after four of the informers he ran were detected and killed by the PIRA.

Many SAS operations were aborted or failed because of measures taken to protect sources. In one operation in Londonderry in the early 1980s, the RUC went so far as to risk one of its own officers being shot in order to maintain the fiction that the Army was responding to the gunfire rather than to source information.

Similarly drastic measures were taken during an operation in Belfast. Source intelligence passed to the local TCG reported that the PIRA were planning to move a large quantity of weapons from a central arms dump in a republican area to a new hide. However, the Army handler insisted that the weapons be allowed to move on through several further locations before being interdicted in order to protect the identity of his source. The Det operators assigned to follow the weapons realised there was a significant chance of losing sight of them in the warren of backstreets in the area and passed their concerns up the chain of command. When the SAS team tasked with the final interdiction complained that an excess of caution might allow the PIRA men to get away, the source handler was unimpressed. The SAS, he observed, just wanted another scalp on their belts but his 'excess of caution' was all that stood between his informant and certain death. The handler's arguments won the day and the weapons were allowed to pass through several different hides. As the Det operators predicted, the trail ultimately went cold and the operation was aborted.

In order to protect their sources and to exploit the growing PIRA paranoia about informers, RUC and military handlers engaged in a game of deception and misdirection. The goal was to convince the PIRA that a completely loyal member of the organisation was responsible for passing information to the security forces. They did this by 'lifting' a terrorist suspect, holding him for a day or so and then releasing him. A short time later, a minor weapons hide would be 'discovered' or an arrest operation carried out, throwing suspicion on the individual who had been arrested. The same man would then be picked up and released the next time the security forces intended to act on more important information from a real source.

This devious tactic sowed the seeds of doubt in the minds of PIRA commanders. It also brought the 'innocent' volunteer under the scrutiny of the PIRA's own internal security unit, known colloquially as the 'nutting squad' for their frequent shooting of suspected informers in the head. Once in the sights of PIRA internal security, a volunteer's fate was often all but sealed. The security forces had an invaluable ally in this deadly game. The head of PIRA internal security in Belfast was, himself, a highly placed informer, code-named 'Stakeknife'. Many PIRA volunteers who were totally innocent of the 'crime' of informing were executed on the orders of their superiors as a result of this disinformation campaign.

Agent handlers knew that their sources, in both loyalist and republican terrorist organisations, would have to continue to engage in terrorist activities if they were to maintain their cover. This often meant that the source himself would need to commit or sanction murders. The morality of such killings, and the degree of British 'complicity' in them, has been fiercely debated in the years since the end of the war in Northern Ireland. What is not in question is the effectiveness of the informer system. Source intelligence was responsible for the loss of many key members of the PIRA and for the almost complete destruction of one of its most active and vicious units, the Tyrone Brigade. Indeed, it is not an exaggeration to say that inside sources were decisive in forcing the PIRA to end its military campaign. By the closing stages of the Troubles, the organisation was so deeply and broadly penetrated by informers that the British security forces knew in advance about three out of every four attacks it tried to mount.

Impressed by the successes of the SAS and 14 Intelligence Company, the RUC decided to set up its own specialised covert units to provide a similar capability that was 'native' to Ulster. An initial attempt to combine surveillance and reaction roles in a single unit led to the creation in 1976 of Bronze Section. However, Bronze Section proved to be too unwieldy a tool for complex operations, so, in 1980, the RUC divided its capabilities. A dedicated surveillance unit, E4A, was formed as a direct mirror of 14 Intelligence Company while a separate reaction force, E4 SSU (Special Support Unit), took on the companion role played by the SAS.

The initial setup of E4A was assisted by operators from 14 Intelligence Company. The new organisation, like its Army counterpart but unlike any other British police unit, had a two-stage selection process. The selection phase took place at Ballykinler Barracks in County Down. This was then followed by an intensive training phase designed to teach all the skills necessary to work as a covert operator.

There were advantages and disadvantages to using E4A officers on surveillance operations instead of soldiers from the Det. The main benefit was that E4A recruits came from the RUC, so the unit was able to draw on a pool of Ulster natives. Also, E4A officers tended to be intimately familiar with the local customs and terrain, and were able to blend into the environment with ease. Furthermore, they could 'speak the language', allowing them to more readily talk their way out of tricky situations. This was a particularly valuable capability since most Det operators could only manage a couple of phrases in an Ulster accent before their cover was blown.

The main disadvantage was that E4A operations were expensive. Police officers, even in specialised units, were only contracted to work an eight-hour day; every further minute was paid as overtime. Det operators, by contrast, were paid a fixed monthly salary regardless of the hours they spent on duty. A surveillance operation lasting several days and involving a large number of E4A operators thus cost far more than a military operation.

The recruitment and training of the SSU was overseen by the SAS. Many ex-servicemen, including marines and paratroopers, were among its first cohort of recruits. The unit was initially used in support of E4A operations in Belfast but it was soon deployed province wide. This led to the SSU becoming involved in a number of controversial shootings.

In late 1982, South TCG received intelligence from a reliable source within the PIRA that around 1,000lbs of weapons and explosives had been smuggled across the border from the Irish Republic. The shipment was being stored in a hayshed near Derrymacash, ten minutes' drive from Kinnego. As well as identifying the location of the cache, the informer also reported that the local PIRA unit was planning to use the explosives to carry out a bomb attack.

A covert search confirmed the accuracy of the information, finding both the explosives and the weapons hidden in the hayshed, so E4A attempted to insert a covert OP to watch the cache but were defeated by the terrain. The farmland around the hayshed was flat and open, and it proved impossible to find sufficient cover in a suitable location nearby. The only alternative was electronic surveillance. A number of movement sensors and microphones were installed in the building and these were then monitored for activity from a remote location. Electronic surveillance capabilities have come a long way in the intervening years, but in the early 1980s they were an imperfect substitute for human eyes on the target. When the local PIRA unit arrived to retrieve the explosives, they went undetected. The result was devastating.

On 27 October 1982, the local RUC were notified about a theft at a farm within the out-of-bounds area set up to cordon off the arms dump. The information was passed up the chain of command. After receiving confirmation from the TCG that the explosives had not been moved, a three-man RUC unit was dispatched to investigate the burglary. As they drove along the Kinnego Embankment towards their destination, a remote control device detonated a 1,000lb bomb that had been planted in a culvert beneath the road. Paul Hamilton, Alan McCloy and Sean Quinn were killed instantly. The crater left by the enormous explosion was some 40 feet wide and reports claim that the RUC car was thrown 70 feet into the air.

That night, the TCG ordered another covert search of the hayshed under cover of darkness. As suspected, the explosives were no longer there. However, three rifles that had not previously been present were discovered in the cache. In the hope of catching the unit responsible for the bombing when they returned to collect their weapons, new sensors and microphones were installed.

The killing of the three RUC officers threw South TCG into turmoil and an emergency meeting was arranged between the original source and his Special Branch handler. Under intense pressure, the source quickly identified the PIRA volunteers responsible for the bombing, leading to 14 Intelligence Company setting up mobile surveillance on the PIRA men. On 11 November 1982, believing the unit was armed and about to carry out another operation, the Det operators called in E4 SSU to intercept them. What happened next has been a subject of controversy ever since.

Three PIRA members – Gervaise McKerr, Eugene Toman and Sean Burns – all of whom were unarmed, were shot dead at a vehicle checkpoint near Lurgan. According to an RUC press statement released shortly afterwards, the car the men were travelling in refused to stop and attempted to run down a police officer. The other officers present, the official report claimed, opened fire in response, killing the occupants of the vehicle. The unit manning the checkpoint was the RUC's SSU. Two weeks later, the sensors in the hayshed alerted the monitoring team that there was activity in the building. The SSU was again dispatched. According to their report, as the officers approached the building, they heard the sounds of weapons being readied and called out for the men inside to surrender. When they received no response, the SSU officers moved into the building, where they were confronted by two young men armed with rifles. Martin McCauley, 19, and Michael Tighe, 17, were both shot. Tighe died at the scene but McCauley was arrested and charged with weapons offences.

During his trial, McCauley denied that any warning was given before the SSU officers opened fire and claimed that he was unarmed and simply looking around the hayshed out of curiosity. He received a two-year suspended sentence for possession of weapons. Twenty-two years after the shootings, McCauley was captured by government forces in Colombia while teaching FARC guerrillas how to use explosives of the type the PIRA had pioneered during the Troubles.

On 12 December 1982, two members of the INLA – Seamus Grew, 30, and Roddy Carroll, 21 – were shot dead by the SSU near Mullacreevie Park in Armagh city. The RUC claimed that the two men had driven through a checkpoint where, as in the Lurgan shootings, the suspects had knocked down a police officer. According to the press statement, they were then pursued 'at speed' before being forced to a halt: 'The driver jumped out of the vehicle and the police, believing they were about to be fired on, themselves opened fire. Both occupants were shot.'

The Armagh and Lurgan shootings bore too many similarities for the fact to pass unnoticed. Under mounting pressure, the RUC re-opened their investigations of the incidents and brought murder charges against four SSU officers. In the Armagh case, Constable John Robinson was charged with the murder of Seamus Grew. The judge acquitted Robinson, accepting his defence that the Constable believed Grew represented a threat to life. However, in the course of the trial Robinson admitted that the initial police statements about the checkpoint and pursuit had been lies intended to conceal the fact that the INLA men were under surveillance. It also emerged that the SSU officers had expected Dominic McGlinchey, the leader of the INLA, to be in the car with the men they killed. Six days prior to the shooting, the INLA had detonated a bomb in the Droppin Well disco in Ballykelly, killing 17. McGlinchey was believed to have ordered the attack.

The three SSU officers accused of murdering Eugene Toman during the Lurgan shooting were acquitted on the same grounds, despite the fact that the IRA men had been unarmed. Lord Justice Gibson commended the officers for their courage and determination, and 'for bringing the three deceased men to justice, in this case, to the final court of justice'. In 1987, a 500lb car bomb killed Lord Gibson. The PIRA claimed responsibility for the murder.

The controversies surrounding the shootings carried out by the SSU led to an official inquiry being set up in 1984 under Deputy Chief Constable John Stalker of the Greater Manchester Police. Stalker's remit was to investigate whether the RUC unit was operating a 'shoot to kill' policy. The findings of the inquiry were never made public. In the aftermath of the shootings, the RUC decided to change the tarnished name of their covert reaction unit to the Headquarters Mobile Support Unit (HMSU).

Quite apart from the public and official unease about the SSU shootings, their activities were also a subject of considerable interest within the ranks of the SAS. The SAS had watched the development of the SSU with some concern, worried that their own role in the province might be usurped by a unit operating on a longer leash and using practices they considered distasteful. Discussions were held at all levels of the regiment in the early 1980s. The SAS came to the conclusion, long before the 'Stalker Inquiry' began, that the tactics used by the SSU were, at the very least, questionable. There was collective agreement that the SAS should not even attempt to adopt them.

The SAS was determined that they should maintain what they considered to be the 'high ground'. Before any terrorists were engaged, the teams on the ground had to be sure that the targets were actively participating in a terrorist incident and, more importantly, that they were armed. This was not purely an ethical matter, despite the advantages for morale of feeling 'in the right'. The tragic killing of John Boyle at Dunloy had convinced the regiment that the last thing they needed was another prosecution of its members in a criminal court. The policy worked and it is a matter of record that for the remaining duration of the covert war in Ulster, no SAS soldier faced criminal prosecution.

CHAPTER SIX

EXPANSION

THE SAS (1980–85)

As the new decade dawned, the RUC's qualms about deploying the SAS on the streets of Belfast were outweighed by the operational requirements of the Belfast TCG. Reliable source intelligence had been received that C Company of the PIRA's Belfast Brigade intended to carry out a sniper attack using a scoped .303 rifle. Det operators, working in conjunction with MI5, located the rifle in a 'hide' in the New Lodge area of the city and fitted the weapon with a tracking device. The TCG tasked the SAS troop in theatre to neutralise the threat.

Conscious that their superiors wanted to avoid the kind of gun battles on the streets that had led to the regiment's exile after the Ballysillan shootings, the Troop offered up a simple, if ruthless, solution. They recommended that the rifle should be booby-trapped, with a small explosive charge placed in the stock. The charge would be activated by the PIRA sniper pulling back the bolt on the rifle, ensuring that the weapon was in use when the terrorist was killed. The SAS had used similar tactics during the recent Dhofar campaign. They argued that the device would be simple to install, that there was little risk to civilian life and that this low-key tactic would result in the elimination of a sniper who had been responsible for a number of security force deaths.

Belfast TCG took the SAS proposal to Army headquarters, where it was immediately quashed, along with the entire operation. Despite the Troop's goal of avoiding an unnecessary firefight, the command staff made it clear that they would not tolerate 'SAS dirty tricks' in Belfast, or in any other area of the province for that matter. The rifle in question was instead lifted by uniformed soldiers in a search operation. The PIRA sniper in question never knew how close he had come to having his head blown off.

Despite this initial setback, the SAS were soon called on for another operation in the city. In the early part of 1980, a PIRA gang had been running rampant in west Belfast, using a belt-fed M60 machine-gun in a number of devastating attacks on the security forces. The M60 Gang, as they were known, became a priority target for the Belfast TCG.

On 2 May 1980, the G Squadron troop currently in theatre received an emergency crash-out order. Information had come into the local TCG that the M60 Gang were on the loose in North Belfast and it was felt that only the SAS had the skills needed to deal with this kind of heavy firepower. 14 Intelligence Company operators picked up the trail of the terrorist team and two unmarked cars containing an eight-man SAS squad headed towards the city from their new base near Lough Neagh. The SAS team commander, Captain Herbert Westmacott, received updated information en route to the target that the gang had taken up position in a house on Antrim Road. A cordon was set up to control entry and exit to the streets around the building.

Captain Westmacott was just beginning to work out a plan of action when he received another report that an unknown car had breached the security perimeter. Believing that the PIRA terrorists had been alerted to the presence of the security forces, he decided on an immediate assault. The SAS team split into two groups. Three men were sent in a car to the rear of the target to cut off any escape. The remaining five men, including Captain Westmacott, formed an assault group and moved to the front of the house in the second vehicle.

As soon as their car came to a halt, the assault group burst out. The PIRA team immediately opened fire with the M60, hitting Captain Westmacott fatally in the head and shoulder. The rest of the assault group returned fire but, finding themselves pinned down in the open by a machine-gun situated in excellent cover, they were forced to make a fighting withdrawal. They carried their fallen commander's body with them as they fell back.

At the rear of the building, the cut-off group apprehended one member of the PIRA team as he prepared a Ford Transit van for the terrorists' escape. The other three PIRA men remained inside. Unwilling to allow Captain Westmacott's death to have been in vain, the remaining members of the assault group prepared for a second attack on the building. As the SAS men readied themselves to storm the building, uniformed members of the security forces began to arrive at the scene, drawn in by the sound of gunfire.

Seeing reinforcements arriving, and fearing the consequences if the SAS made another assault, the PIRA unit pushed their M60 out of the window and ran up a white flag. Much to the disgust and disappointment of the SAS team, the terrorists were taken into custody unharmed.

Captain Westmacott was the first member of the SAS to lose his life in combat in Ulster. He was posthumously awarded the Military Cross for gallantry. The three captured terrorists – Angelo Fusco, Paul Magee and Joe Doherty – escaped from custody before they could be brought to trial. In June 1981, they were convicted of murder in absentia.

The SAS learned a hard lesson from the death of Captain Westmacott. A half-troop had neither enough men nor sufficient firepower to carry out an immediate assault on a building containing well-armed terrorists. Heavy casualties for the attacking force were almost inevitable under such circumstances. The SAS would never again make the mistake of sending in units that lacked the capabilities required to complete the task at hand. In the future, daylight frontal assaults would only be undertaken by a full SAS anti-terrorist team acting in accordance with a prepared plan.

In September 1980, following South TCG receiving intelligence concerning the location of an arms cache hidden in a henhouse in a staunchly republican area of Tyrone, 14 Intelligence Company undertook a covert search and discovered a concealed sniper rifle. The next night, an MI5 Weapons Intelligence Unit

(WIU), guarded by an SAS team, visited the cache and made the weapon safe.

With the rifle disarmed, the SAS set up an ambush on the location and waited. Several nights later, Francis Quinn and Thomas Hamill, both leading members of the PIRA's North Armagh Brigade, arrived at the henhouse. The SAS team waited until the weapon was retrieved and then apprehended both men. Quinn and Hamill were later tried and sentenced to eight years in prison for possession of the rifle.

In early January 1981, Mid Ulster TCG received hard intelligence that a loyalist group intended to assassinate Bernadette McAliskey, better known by her maiden name as Bernadette Devlin. Devlin was a controversial leader of the Catholic civil rights movement and was much despised by hardline loyalists. She had risen to prominence first as a student leader and then as the youngest Member of Parliament when she won the Mid Ulster seat in 1969 at the age of 21. Later the same year, she was involved in the so-called Battle of the Bogside, the first major riots of the Troubles. In the aftermath, she was convicted on three counts of incitement to riot and sentenced to six months in prison.

Devlin remained a powerful independent force in the republican movement throughout the 1970s, working with various groups, including the political wing of the INLA. She was also one of the few members of the movement who could claim to have laid hands on a British government minister. The day after the Bloody Sunday shootings in 1972, Devlin, who had been in the crowd when British troops opened fire, was present in the House of Commons for a statement from the Home Secretary. Devlin challenged the minister's claim that the British soldiers were responding to gunfire, twice calling him a liar and stating that 'Nobody shot at the paratroops, but somebody will shortly'. Eventually, when the Speaker of the House refused to allow her to speak, she walked across the aisle and slapped the Home Secretary across the face.

The intelligence received by Mid Ulster TCG was that a loyalist assassination squad from the South Belfast UDA planned to attack Devlin in her home near Coalisland, County Tyrone. The troop in theatre, detached from D Squadron, was tasked to carry out a covert surveillance of the location and prepare an ambush to interdict the gunmen if they arrived. As was common practice, the men adopted the uniforms of a local army unit, the 3rd Battalion of the Parachute Regiment.

On 16 January 1981, Ray Smallwoods, Tom Graham and Andrew Watson, all members of the South Belfast UDA, arrived by car at the secluded farmhouse where Devlin lived. The attack happened at the worst possible time. The men in the covert OP were in the process of handing over to their relief and for a few brief minutes their eyes were taken off the building. It was only when they heard the sound of gunfire that the waiting SAS team was alerted to the attack. Two of the gunmen, Smallwoods and Graham, had broken into the farmhouse and shot Devlin fourteen times as her children listened. Devlin's husband, Michael McAliskey, was also shot.

On hearing the shooting, the SAS team moved in and secured the building. All three UDA terrorists were apprehended as they attempted to escape. Each man later received a long jail term. The SAS medic present gave Devlin and her husband first aid, which undoubtedly saved their lives, while other members of the Troop arranged for a medevac helicopter.

Unsurprisingly, republican conspiracy theorists began to propagate the story that the Army deliberately delayed acting in order to allow the loyalist gunmen to kill their target. Devlin herself contributed to the misinformation, claiming that the 'paratroops' had left her untended on the floor of her kitchen for half an hour and had been slow in calling for the evacuation in the hope she would die.

The truth, as always, is more straightforward. The fact that Devlin survived 14 gunshots should, by itself, be enough to debunk the claim that the SAS team withheld treatment. Had they done so, she would certainly have died. The suggestion that the team allowed the attack to happen in the first place is harder to disprove but there is not a shred of evidence to support it beyond hostile speculation. The unfortunate reality is that operations in the field are complex, messy affairs and subject to all sorts of unpredictable factors. Devlin's shooting was simply a product of bad luck and bad timing, rather than any deliberate inaction on the behalf of the SAS team. Professional as they are, it is worth remembering that the SAS are fallible. The Troop commander responsible for the operation, who was later awarded an MBE, knew full well how easily mistakes could be made. He was one of the unfortunate men who had strayed across the border in 1975 and been arrested and charged by the Irish police.

Throughout 1980 and into the early part of 1981, a PIRA ASU headed by Seamus McElwaine had been increasingly active in County Fermanagh. McElwaine was one of the deadliest killers produced by the Troubles. In 1980 alone, he is known to have murdered at least two off-duty members of the security forces, Corporal Aubrey Abercrombie of the UDR and Constable Ernest Johnston of the RUC Reserve. RUC Special Branch and MI5 possessed reliable intelligence that he had been involved in at least another ten killings. At the age of just nineteen, McElwaine's ruthlessness saw him elevated to the command of the PIRA's Fermanagh Brigade.

Eliminating McElwaine became a priority for the Mid Ulster TCG and, to this end, the local Det was tasked with carrying out extensive surveillance of anyone associated with him. On 14 March 1981, the surveillance operation finally bore fruit when McElwaine and three other PIRA members were observed entering a farmhouse near the village of Rosslea in County Fermanagh. The PIRA men were heavily-armed, carrying an Armalite, a Heckler and Koch assault rifle, an M1 carbine and a Ruger rifle, as well as a large quantity of ammunition.

After the report was called in by 14 Intelligence Company, the SAS troop in theatre crashed out in response. The farmhouse was quickly surrounded and planning began. The G Squadron men considered and rejected the idea of an immediate assault, having learned the lesson of Captain Westmacott's death the previous year. The anti-terrorist team in Hereford was put on standby in case a full-scale assault became necessary but the men on the ground decided to try a more direct approach first.

The Sergeant Major in charge of the SAS team walked out into the open in full view of the PIRA terrorists and loudly informed them that the farmhouse was surrounded. Unless they surrendered within ten minutes, he announced, his men would blast the encircled terrorists out with grenades. The trapped PIRA men came out with their hands up in less than five minutes.

Since the Antrim Road debacle, the SAS had, without official sanction, deployed American-made fragmentation grenades to the Troop in Ulster. The G Squadron assault team undoubtedly had such weapons in their possession. Whether or not they would have used them, and what the political ramifications would have been if they did, will never be known. The presence of the grenades may have been politically questionable but, despite never being used at any time during the Troubles, the author can attest that they provided considerable comfort to the men deployed in theatre.

McElwaine and four other PIRA members (the fourth of whom had been arrested at another location and tied by fingerprint evidence to the weapons seized) subsequently faced trial. McElwaine was convicted of the murders of Corporal Abercrombie and Reserve Constable Johnstone, with the trial judge recommending that he serve at least thirty years in prison for his crimes. Just eighteen months into his sentence, on 23 September 1983,

McElwaine took part in a mass breakout of PIRA prisoners from the Maze Prison. He and the SAS would meet again.

The SAS suffered its third fatality in Northern Ireland on 8 February 1983, when Corporal Thomas 'Tommy' Palmer was killed in a car crash at a roundabout near Lurgan. Tommy Palmer was a veteran of the Dhofar campaign and had been awarded the Queen's Gallantry Medal for his actions at the 1980 London Iranian Embassy siege, during which he killed two of the six-man terrorist team. A larger-than-life character, Palmer was popular throughout the SAS and his loss was felt keenly by all members of the regiment.

In July 1984, Mid Ulster TCG received credible intelligence from a technical source that the PIRA's Tyrone Brigade intended to attack a factory using incendiary bombs. The intelligence indicated that up to four terrorists would be involved and that they would be carrying firearms as well as bombs. The troop in theatre, from D Squadron, was tasked to insert a covert OP and deployed an eight-man team to intercept the bombers.

The team deployed to the target location at 23.10 on 13 July, splitting into two three-man groups and one two-man group to maximise coverage of possible approach routes. Fifteen minutes after moving into position, a corporal covering one of the approaches caught sight of movement. He watched through the night scope of his Armalite as two armed men appeared near the factory. Seconds later, the pair were joined by another two men and at 23.30, the ASU began to head towards their target. All four men moved at a slow, stealthy crouch, unaware they were already in the gun-sights of the SAS.

The corporal passed word to the other two ambush groups that the armed terrorists were approaching. He waited until it was clear that the men could not be heading anywhere other than the factory and then called out a challenge. The leading PIRA man raised one of his hands in response and was immediately shot four times by the corporal. The other three terrorists turned and fled back the way they had come, fortunate to have chosen the only route out that didn't take them through the fields of fire of the other SAS ambush groups.

The dead PIRA man was later named as Volunteer William Price from Ardboe in County Tyrone, the son of a former British Army soldier. A .455 Smith and Wesson revolver, of the type carried by officers during the First World War, was found under his body with five rounds in the cylinder. Another discarded pistol was later recovered by an RUC forensic investigation team that attended the scene.

This was a classic SAS operation based upon sound intelligence and carried out with professionalism and bravery by the soldiers involved. The SAS corporal who shot Price was awarded the Military Medal for his actions and later served with distinction in the Falklands War.

The undercover war was fought in a myriad of backstreets and hedgerows across the province. This book chronicles the major incidents. But for every operation that ended in the capture or death of a terrorist, there were hundreds that did not. Operations could fail for many different reasons. Faulty or incomplete intelligence was one common cause of fruitless days and nights spent shivering in fields or trying to look inconspicuous in civilian cars. More surprisingly, perhaps, bad discipline among the terrorists was another reason that many operations yielded no results. Volunteers, often young men with poor work records who had undergone little formal training, would frequently get drunk rather than move weapons on a cold night. At other times, men failed to turn up for planned operations simply because they were unmotivated or scared. It is an irony of the undercover war that one of the principle reasons for the 'failure' of SAS operations was that the terrorist targets often failed in their own missions before even starting.

When not active on operations, SAS personnel filled their time with fitness training and CQB practice at the Army ranges in Ballykinler. Ambushes and car intercepts were simulated under every conceivable set of conditions, day and night and in all weathers. Anti-ambush drills were practiced until every man could carry them out in his sleep. However, despite the intensive training regimen, it was impossible to anticipate every contingency that might arise in a fast-moving operation.

A favourite tactic of republican terrorists was to target off-duty members of the RUC and UDR when they were at their most vulnerable. Among the most dangerous assignments that could be given to a member of the Troop in Ulster was to act as a substitute or decoy, standing in for a member of the security forces who had been targeted for assassination. Those who volunteered for such missions required the coolest of heads, as well as steel in another part of the anatomy.

One such operation took place in October 1984, when the Mid Ulster TCG received reliable intelligence from an informer that a UDR major had been targeted for assassination. The source reported that the officer would be attacked near the largely Protestant town of Portadown while driving to work.

One of the Troop members, Corporal Alistair Slater of B Squadron, bore a striking resemblance in both height and weight to the intended target. 'Big Al', as Corporal Slater was known in the Troop, agreed without hesitation when asked if he would be willing to take the place of the intended target. A second SAS man, Frank 'Ginge' Collins, volunteered to secrete himself in the back of the target's car in order to provide close protection for the vulnerable decoy.

The remaining members of the Troop were divided into three-man teams, with one team in each of three civilian cars. The job of driving the cars was assigned to those best able to handle manoeuvring at speed. One of the picked drivers, Corporal Nish Bruce, was well known in the unit for his intuitive and accurate fast-driving skills. The plan was for the three cars to shadow Al Slater's vehicle and allow the PIRA terrorists to initiate their attack. Once the attack began, the SAS teams would step in and eliminate the threat.

On the night of 18 August 1984, a PIRA ASU wearing green boiler suits took over a house in Washington Road, Coalisland. The owner, Daniel McIntyre, was held hostage overnight. When the PIRA team left the next morning, they took with them McIntyre's yellow van. McIntyre was warned not to report the incident until at least 10.30 a.m.

With a 'clean' vehicle in their possession, the assassination team now moved to intercept what they believed to be their unsuspecting target. The ASU pulled the van over to the side of the road near a petrol station at Verner's Bridge and waited for their intended victim. As Al Slater's car approached their position, the PIRA terrorists lowered the back window in the van and prepared to open fire.

Corporal Slater was scanning the road ahead for potential threats when he spotted the suspiciously parked vehicle up ahead. He quickly radioed in its location and slowed his car down to a crawl, not wanting to approach the likely ambush site too closely. The PIRA terrorists knew that security forces personnel were often wary of possible dangers when driving due to the high frequency of assassination attempts. Seeing the target car slow down, they decided to lull their victim into a false sense of security. The van moved slowly off from its parked position and then took a right turn onto a road that passed under a bridge. Corporal Slater drove past the turnoff in an attempt to get a good visual identification of the suspect vehicle and then continued along his planned route. The PIRA men now turned their van around and returned to the road, hoping to come up with their target from the rear and surprise him.

Alerted by Corporal Slater's radio call, the circling SAS teams moved in. The first car to arrive was driven by Nish Bruce, who closed with the terrorist vehicle from behind. Realising that their operation was blown, the PIRA terrorists opened fire on their pursuer through the back windows of the van, triggering a fast-moving gun battle along narrow and twisting country lanes.

One member of the pursuit team recalls the weight of fire that was poured out at them as being like 'a sheet of lead'. Despite the hail of rounds flying around him, Corporal Bruce didn't flinch or hang back for a moment. Instead, he kept his car right up on the tail of the fleeing van, remaining as close as was reasonably possible.

The SAS men suffered from a significant disadvantage in this almost cinematic firefight. The country lanes through which the pursuit took place were frequently so narrow that the Troop members were unable to lean out of the car windows to shoot at the PIRA van. Instead they had to resort to the dangerous expedient of shooting through the laminated windows of their own car. Unfortunately, this resulted in the rounds being 'stripped' of the protective metal jacket that covers the soft lead of the bullets used in military rifles. As a result, none of the bullets were able to do decisive damage to their targets. The PIRA team, on the other hand, were able to avoid this problem by simply removing the rear window in the van.

As the high-speed chase continued, the other two SAS cars managed to get ahead of the van with the goal of bringing it to a halt by boxing it in. Seeing what the SAS team intended, one of the terrorists leaped into the front passenger seat and immediately opened fire on the cars ahead. The SAS men returned fire but in the moving chaos of swerving vehicles and shattered glass, none of their rounds managed to stop the van or its driver. In a desperate attempt to escape, the PIRA van swerved sharply and took a turn that led back towards the area from which the van had originally been stolen.

The sudden and surprising manoeuvre gained the PIRA team a few vital seconds. The time it took for the SAS cars to follow was just enough for the terrorists to reach a cul-de-sac, park the vehicle temporarily out of sight and make their escape into the surrounding streets on foot. As the SAS teams arrived and jumped out of their cars, one soldier opened fire on the retreating men. Tragically, an innocent civilian, Frederick Jackson, was killed by one of the bullets.

The abandoned van was later examined by RUC forensic teams. Inside, they found a discarded shotgun, a CB radio and dozens of empty cases fired from automatic weapons. Later that day, the PIRA team made their way to a safe house. Unbeknown to them, the location had been compromised. An MI5 listening device, unfortunately not monitored in real-time, recorded the conversation between the men. Quite naturally, the main topic of discussion was who had sprung the trap. One member of the ASU suggested that it must have been the SAS. Another replied, *'No. If it was the SAS we'd all be dead.'* Sometimes reputations can outrun reality.

Nish Bruce was awarded the Queen's Gallantry Medal for his unflinching bravery in maintaining the pursuit of the van while under almost continual fire. Nish was one of the leading free fall parachute experts in the British Army. After leaving the SAS, he was involved in highly dangerous trials to develop a suit that would enable Space Shuttle astronauts to free fall to earth from near outer space. In the years after he left the Army, Nish was plagued by severe mental health issues, a struggle he documented under the pseudonym of Tom Read in his book *Freefall*. Nish committed suicide on 8 January 2002, throwing himself from a light aircraft without a parachute in one final free-fall jump.

Frank 'Ginge' Collins, who had volunteered to hide in the back of the decoy vehicle, was another victim of the mental health difficulties that face many Special Forces soldiers when they return to civilian life. Frank was a committed Christian and became a priest after leaving the SAS. He served as an Army Chaplin with the Territorial 23 SAS Regiment (Reserve) and then later with the Parachute Regiment. He was forced out of the Army after writing his autobiography, *Baptism of Fire*. A year later, in 1998, for reasons no one really knows, Frank took his own life.

On the night of 1 December 1984, Mid Ulster TCG received intelligence that local PIRA units intended to carry out a gun and bomb attack in the Kesh area of County Fermanagh. The intelligence was sketchy and imprecise; the only hard fact given was that a blue Toyota van would be involved in some way.

At about 00.25 on 2 December, the duty officer in the RUC station at Kesh received a phone call. A female voice calmly informed him that the Fermanagh Brigade of the IRA had planted a number of incendiary bombs in the Drumrush Lodge, a local hotel. The reason the hotel was being targeted, she said, was because its owners were willing to serve 'the bastard security forces'.

Mid Ulster TCG considered the two pieces of intelligence they now had and concluded, correctly, that the Fermanagh PIRA had set up an ambush in the area. The telephone call to Kesh police station was a 'come on' designed to lure a police or army patrol out into the trap. What the TCG did not know was that a few hours earlier, a five-man PIRA unit had hijacked a blue Toyota van in the village of Pettigo, across the border in County Donegal. The family who owned the van were taken hostage and a PIRA gunman remained with them as the vehicle was driven off. Shortly after midnight, the rest of the ASU returned. Before leaving, they warned the family not to report the incident for at least two and a half hours.

All but one of the terrorists were dressed in military-style combat uniforms. The fifth, Antoine Mac Giolla Bhrighde, also known as Tony MacBride, was dressed in civilian clothes. In 1972, when MacBride was just 14 years old, two loyalist terror- ists had attempted to murder his father in a sectarian shooting. MacBride was present and was hit by one of the bullets. His father was shot fourteen times and died a year later, having never recovered. The death of his father and the attempt on his own life is most likely what motivated the young man to join the Provisional IRA. MacBride moved south to the Republic, where he acquired professional military experience in the Irish Army before deserting. In 1979, he was arrested for possession of a rifle and sentenced to three years in prison. By 1984, he was a seasoned, dedicated terrorist.

Mid Ulster TCG crashed out the B Squadron troop in theatre. The Troop moved quickly towards Kesh in civilian vehicles, three men to a car. They were determined to arrive in time to disrupt the PIRA operation.

As the SAS teams made their way towards Kesh, the PIRA ASU prepared their ambush. A landmine, consisting of beer kegs filled with explosives, was placed in a culvert under the entrance to the driveway of the hotel. The plan was to run a command wire to a safe position where a firing team had concealed themselves. The culvert bomb would be detonated when the security force patrol arrived in response to the warning call. The ASU would then shoot any survivors. Had the ambush succeeded, it would have been a massacre.

A thick mist covered the whole area when the first SAS car, driven by the redoubtable Al Slater, arrived at the scene. The events that followed need to be understood in the context of the limited information available to the SAS team. The men knew about the warning call to Kesh police station and that the TCG believed the call to be a 'come on'. They also knew that the TCG believed a gun and bomb attack was being prepared by the PIRA and that a blue van might be involved. Beyond these basic details, they would have to work things out as they went along.

As Corporal Slater drove through the twisting roads leading up to the Drumrush Lodge Hotel, he noticed a blue Toyota parked on a side road as he passed. He continued driving down the road until he had reached what he felt was a safe distance and then pulled his car to a halt alongside a hedgerow. The three-man team in the vehicle got out of their car to assess the situation.

The SAS men had no idea that they had stopped almost immediately alongside the PIRA firing team. Nor were the PIRA terrorists aware of the nearby enemy presence. It was as if the heavy fog formed an impenetrable wall between the two units, obscuring vision and deadening all sound.

As the SAS men discussed what to do next, a figure appeared out of the fog from the direction of the hotel, hunched over and walking towards them with a strange gait. Tony MacBride was returning to the firing position from the bomb site, unravelling the command wire that was to allow the remote detonation of the culvert bomb. Corporal Slater called out a challenge to the unknown man but due to the effects of the fog, MacBride couldn't hear what was said. Assuming the words had come from another member of his own ASU, he replied, *'Hush! It's me!'* Corporal Slater repeated his challenge, only to hear the same response in return. Unwilling to allow the mysterious figure to close any further, Slater called out as loud as he could: *'Stop! Security forces!'* This time the message went home. MacBride dropped the command wire and disappeared at a run back into the fog. As the driver of the car, Slater stayed with the vehicle while his two passengers set off down the road in pursuit.

In order to do whatever he could to assist in the chase, Corporal Slater moved to the rear of his vehicle and took out a parachute flare from the boot of the car. With the launcher in hand, he fired, lighting up the surrounding area with an eerie phosphorescent glow. This act cost him his life. A moment later, the PIRA team opened fire as a target flashed into visibility immediately in front of them. Al was hit instantly. Despite his grave wounds, he managed to return fire at the enemy position. But outnumbered, outgunned and in poor cover, there was little he could do. The ASU concentrated their fire on their target and, a few moments later, Al fell to the ground, mortally wounded. The PIRA firing team then began to withdraw.

While the firefight was taking place by the car, the two other members of the SAS team caught up with MacBride and arrested him. MacBride was wearing two pairs of trousers, the inner pair black and the outer pair green, as well as a black hooded anorak and army-style boots. The two SAS men quickly realised they had captured a PIRA terrorist.

Due to the strange atmospherics caused by the fog, the sounds of gunfire did not reach the soldiers as they chased down MacBride. They returned to the car completely oblivious to the fact that a contact had been fought out in their absence. As they approached the vehicle, the shocking sight of Al Slater's unmoving body came into view. One of the men passed his rifle to the other and rushed over to administer first aid. Seeing his chance, MacBride attempted to grab the weapon and was shot dead.

The remaining members of the retreating PIRA ASU had not planned a withdrawal on foot. They made their way through the thick fog to the Bannagh River. Seeing no other options, they attempted a crossing. Deep pools dotting the riverbed were invisible under the surface. PIRA Volunteer Kieran Fleming stepped into one of these holes and disappeared beneath the waters. His body was found the next day.

Al Slater was posthumously awarded the Military Medal for gallantry. He was the fourth, and last, member of the SAS to die in Northern Ireland. Al had found a little local fame when he appeared as a Training Platoon Instructor on the BBC's 1983 documentary series, *The Paras*. He was also a talented runner, successfully completing the Belfast Marathon in under three hours. One of his favourite stories to tell in the mess was about that marathon. As he turned onto the Falls Road stretch of the course, some of those in the crowd recognised him from the TV. The last thing he expected to hear in such a staunchly republican area was encouraging shouts of '*Up the Paras!*' from the Catholic youths lining the road. Al was a warm and funny man who was immensely popular throughout the regiment. The author of this book has no shame in admitting that when he heard of Al's death, he cried.

B Squadron's tour in Ulster had been highly eventful. The troop from G Squadron who took their place arrived hoping for similar levels of action. Much to their chagrin, they instead faced a lull in operations. Intelligence was slow to come in and the little that was passed to the SAS was of a low quality and unlikely to generate meaningful actions. In an attempt to stay busy, the Troop decided to turn themselves into targets and invite the PIRA to come out and play.

A large number of commercial vehicles were, at this time, being hijacked in South Armagh by the Crossmaglen unit of the PIRA. Taking note of this, the Troop obtained a similar truck for themselves, lined it with sandbags and placed an ambush party inside. The vehicle was then parked at a truck stop near the town. The ambush party waited several days in the hope that an ASU would try to steal their truck but the PIRA refused to bite. The operation was cancelled and the men went back to fitness regimes, CQB training and otherwise twiddling their thumbs.

The lull was not to last. The SAS was about to begin their most intensive and devastating series of operations against the PIRA, fuelled by information from the most unlikely of sources.

CHAPTER SEVEN

DEATH OF A HERO

THE DET (1980–85)

The 1980s saw little let up in the intensity of Det operations, despite the emergence in the RUC of their sister unit, E4A. During this period, the Det was instrumental in preventing many major terrorist outrages. The constant flow of information from the Det's surveillance operations in republican areas allowed an increasingly sophisticated picture to be built up of the activities of the terrorist groups. Direct surveillance was now complemented by more frequent and accurate reports from informers inside the terrorist groups, as well as information from new technical sources, such as electronic 'bugs' and phone intercepts.

Successful Det operations resulted in weapons being lifted, bombs being intercepted, or target individuals being located. However, the simple fact that operators were working in close proximity with armed and increasingly surveillance-aware terrorists meant that clashes were inevitable. The primary function of

Det operators was the gathering of intelligence; contacts, when they happened, were always the result of unplanned and unexpected occurrences, caused either by bad luck or by an operator pushing boundaries during an operation.

In late May 1981, tensions in the republican areas of Londonderry were high. Patsy O'Hara, a hunger-striker with roots in the city, had died on the twenty-first of that month. Intelligence poured into the Londonderry TCG that the PIRA were planning a major retaliatory strike against security forces in the city.

At about 11.30 on the morning of 28 May, Daniel Moore was driving his car along Iniscarn Road in the Creggan area of Londonderry, when another car containing four masked men pulled up beside him and forced him to stop. A terrorist wearing combat clothes and a balaclava got out of the vehicle with a rifle in his hands and informed the terrified civilian that they were 'borrowing' his car and he would get it back later. Moore was then driven to another location and locked in a shed for an hour and a half before being released.

Neither Londonderry TCG nor Londonderry Det knew about the hijacking of Moore's car but information soon began to pour in from a range of sources that a heavily-armed, four-man PIRA ASU was mobile in the city, looking for a security force target. No one knew what the target was but it was clear the threat was imminent.

All Det operators were scrambled in an attempt to locate the assassination team. Every available car was deployed, with one exception: a brown Opel that had been actively spotted and targeted by PIRA members the previous day. The car had been 'blown', as the phrase went in surveillance circles, and all operators were warned not to use it. However, on finding that no other vehicle was available, one operator decided to risk taking the Opel out rather than be left behind. In doing so, he ignored both standard operating procedures and the most basic good sense. The decision nearly cost him his life and resulted in one of the most spectacular close-range shootings of the entire undercover war.

As the Det operator drove the compromised vehicle along Lone Moor Road, he spotted a brown Ford Escort with four men in it coming in the opposite direction. Once the occupants were within visual range, he quickly identified the men as known PIRA terrorists and radioed in their location, suspecting that he had located the mobile ASU. As the terrorist car passed on the other side of the road, the operator was aware of the occupants staring at him.

For their part, the PIRA team was no less quick to recognise the brown Opel as the vehicle that had been spotted acting suspiciously the day before. The PIRA driver swiftly put his car about and set off in pursuit. As the Opel approached the junction of Coach Road, the terrorist car overtook it and, horn blaring, forced it over to the side of the road.

One of the PIRA men, Eamon McCourt, leaped out of the Escort armed with an Armalite and ran to the front of the Det operator's car. A second man, George McBrearty, ran to the rear similarly armed to cut off the Opel's escape. A third terrorist,

Charles Maguire, then approached the driver-side door with a pistol in his hand.

The Det operator was later to tell his colleagues that, at that moment, he was sure he was about to die. A strange calm came over him. In the expanded seconds of the mind's adrenaline-fuelled response to lethal danger he determined two things: first, there was no way he was going to allow himself to be captured, and second, he was going to take at least one of the terrorists with him.

As Maguire moved carefully towards the car door with his weapon at the ready, the operator wound down his window as if to speak to the approaching man. Secreted in a holster attached to the door was a cocked and ready Browning 9mm pistol with an extended twenty-round magazine. The moment Maguire leaned forward to talk, the operator drew the Browning, released the safety and shot the terrorist twice in the head through the open car window.

At the front of the vehicle, Eamon McCourt immediately responded to the gunshots by opening fire with an automatic burst from his high-velocity rifle. The .223 rounds smashed through the front window of the car but missed their intended target. Instead of hitting the driver, they passed along the length of the vehicle, exited through the rear window and slammed into the waiting McBrearty, killing him instantly. While McCourt struggled to control the recoil of his rifle and bring it back into line, the operator switched to his new target and fired through the shattered glass. McCourt was hit five times. With the three nearest targets all down, the operator snapped off two shots at the final terrorist, still in the driving seat of the Escort, but missed. Unwilling to tempt fate further, the operator slammed his car into reverse and made good his escape.

Maguire, McBrearty and McCourt were driven away from the scene by their uninjured compatriot. McCourt was subsequently taken to a local hospital by ambulance, where he was treated and survived his injuries. He was later sentenced to five years' imprisonment after pleading guilty to attempted hijacking and possession of two rifles with intent.

As often happened, the shootings set off a chain of further incidents. An RUC patrol responding to reports of the hijacking was itself shot at and returned fire. Later that night, there was rioting in both the Creggan and Bogside areas of the city. The operator who had so nearly lost his life was severely reprimanded for taking a blown car out in breach of operating procedures. He was also awarded the Military Cross for bravery in the face of the enemy.

In February 1983, another shooting involving a member of 14 Intelligence Company occurred in Londonderry. The operator in question, Paul Oram, can without exaggeration be described as a legend in British Special Forces circles. Oram had joined the Det from the 9th/12th Royal Lancers and was now back with the unit on his second deployment. He was a family man in his late twenties, solidly built and with a belly that attested to his fondness for a few beers when off-duty. During his time with the Det, Oram had survived several close brushes with death and many in the unit believed that he led a charmed life. He had been awarded a

Mention in Dispatches on his first deployment, been promoted to Sergeant and was considered by all to be one of the top operators in the unit.

On 22 February 1983, Londonderry TCG received intelligence from an informer that a wanted INLA terrorist named Neil McMonagle had entered the city from the Republic of Ireland. The source reported that McMonagle intended to retrieve a rifle from a 'hide' and use it to carry out an attack against an unknown security force target. McMonagle was well known to the security forces. Despite being just twenty-three years old, he had already served four years in prison for robbery, theft and possession of a firearm and was suspected of involvement in the bombing of the El Greco nightclub.

The intelligence source indicated that the weapons cache McMonagle intended to use was somewhere in Leafair Park, part of the Shantallow estate. The Shantallow estate was a die-hard republican area and one of the most hostile environments for Londonderry's Det to operate within. The source was unable to give an exact location for the hide but had narrowed the possibilities down to a number of suspect houses in a small area. Paul Oram's mission on the night of the second was to undertake a 'walk past' of these houses in order to identify any suspicious activity and 'house' McMonagle and any other suspects. Once the location had been established, further surveillance was planned with the goal of eventually launching an organised arrest operation.

Oram drove to the area and parked up. He knew that while operating alone and on foot in a hostile area was perilous enough, walking past a potentially active terrorist cell magnified the danger tenfold. Other members of the Londonderry Det were patrolling nearby in satellite cars but there was a limit to how close the support units could be without blowing the operation. The chances of backup arriving in time if things went wrong were slim.

In order to blend in, Oram was dressed in a duffle coat and jeans for the walk past. His only personal protection was the Browning 9mm pistol with an extended magazine that served as the standard defensive weapon of Det operators. Oram disliked pistol holsters of any kind, seeing them as unnecessary and bulky encumbrances, and preferred to tuck his weapon into the waistband at the rear of his trousers. On this night, however, due to the difficulty of retrieving a pistol from the rear under a long duffle coat, he decided to carry his Browning in the waistband at the front instead. That decision was to save his life.

Oram began his first walk past of the houses, moving at a casual pace and scanning the buildings using his peripheral vision. Passing the first suspect houses, he was unable to see any suspicious activity that might help identify the location of the hide. But as he emerged from an alleyway near another of the potential locations, he caught sight of a known INLA terrorist by the name of Liam Duffy. Duffy was walking towards the same alleyway Oram had just exited, so Oram turned away from the INLA man and walked around the block until he found a safe location. Then he made radio contact with his base. He informed the base unit that he had sighted Duffy but had not been able to 'house' him. Oram's handlers requested a second walk past to try to confirm the suspect location. Despite the obvious dangers involved, he agreed.

On his second circuit, Oram again passed Liam Duffy in the street and formed the strong impression that the INLA man had come from the nearest of the suspect buildings. He returned to the safe location and contacted base again. By this time, both Oram and the base unit were deeply concerned that Duffy might have spotted him and that his cover had been blown. Unwilling to risk the life of an operator, the base unit advised him to pull out. Oram, however, had other ideas. He suspected he had nearly 'housed' Duffy on the previous run, so, in the hope of securely confirming the location, he decided to carry out a third walk past.

Setting off down the street, Oram forced himself to maintain a relaxed walking pace despite the danger of the situation. As he passed the target house, he heard a sudden shout behind him. He turned to see Duffy standing a dozen or so paces away, calling for him to come over. Oram gave a flat, disinterested reply and kept walking, hoping that if he made no sudden moves he might allay the terrorist's suspicion that he was anything other than a local out for a walk. The hope was in vain. Rather than let the suspicious walker go, Duffy rushed up behind Oram, grabbing him by the shoulder with one hand and pushing a pistol hard into his back with the other. Using the pressure from the pistol to steer him towards a nearby fence, Duffy's left hand ran up and down Oram's back, searching for a weapon. Oram glanced over his shoulder to see the target of the operation, Neil McMonagle, advancing towards him with an M1 carbine in what soldiers call the 'high port' position.

Oram knew that if he allowed himself to be pushed up against the fence, he was as good as dead. His only hope now was to seize the initiative and take control of the situation. With a quick turn, Oram slid past the pistol in his back and slammed his substantial body hard up against Duffy, sending the INLA man tumbling to the ground. Without pausing, he drew his Browning and snapped off two quick shots at the advancing McMonagle, dropping him to the ground, then pivoted and fired another two rounds down at Duffy before the terrorist could recover and bring his own weapon to bear. Not knowing whether there were any other threats in the vicinity, Oram sprinted from the contact area as fast as he could, recovered his car and accelerated away to safety.

Neil McMonagle died at the scene and was later given a full paramilitary funeral. Liam Duffy survived thanks to the medical aid given to him by the Army medics who were part of the reaction force called in after the shooting. Duffy was arrested, charged with firearms offences and later convicted. Rioting broke out in Londonderry that night in response to the shooting.

Paul Oram's near-miraculous escape earned him the admiration of both the Det and the SAS Troop members who were currently in the province. In order to celebrate his achievements, his colleagues 'dined him out' in style. At the conclusion of the rather liquid 'dinner', the assembled soldiers called on the man of the moment to give a toast. Paul, much the worse for the considerable amount of alcohol he had consumed, staggered to his feet.

He pointed to one group in the crowd and declared, '*Paras ... Overrated!*' Then, pointing to another group, he shouted out, '*Marines ... Overrated!*' The finger of judgement next turned to the Troop members present. '*SAS ... Overrated!*' Finally, Oram looked down and patted his own ample stomach, which had felled an armed terrorist and bought him the time he needed to escape. In a voice laden with the wisdom of the ages, he pronounced solemnly, '*Deadly bellies kill.*' The remark brought the house down. Paul Oram was awarded the Military Medal for bravery for his actions that night on the Shantallow estate.

In late November 1983, information from a highly-placed informer inside the PIRA alerted Mid-Ulster TCG that an ASU in the Dungannon area of County Tyrone was about to launch an operation against an off-duty member of the security forces. Mid-Ulster Det was tasked to run a surveillance operation in the area.

Before launching an operation, the PIRA would use 'dickers', unarmed members of the ASU or local youths who aspired to join, to look for any security force activity in the area. It is believed that in this case the dickers observed a number of unidentified cars moving about the location of the intended assassination and, as a result, on 1 December, the ASU called off the operation and dumped their weapons in a small field. As the weapons were being concealed, one of the men accidentally discharged a shotgun. The shot was heard by the Det surveillance team waiting nearby so they moved towards the noise, hoping to get eyes on the PIRA team. By the time the Det operators reached the weapons cache, the ASU had already left, so it was decided that the operators would remain and 'stake out' the area in the hope that someone would come to retrieve the weapons.

Around 3 p.m. on Sunday, 4 December, a brown Talbot car pulled up next to the field and two men, PIRA volunteers Brian Campbell and Colm McGirr, got out. McGirr entered the field through a gap in the surrounding hedge and went straight to the hidden arms cache. He knelt down and pulled out the Armalite rifle concealed there, handing it over to Campbell. Campbell turned and headed back towards the car with the rifle while McGirr, still kneeling, pulled out the concealed shotgun.

At this point, a Det member broke cover and moved towards the weapons cache. As he neared it, he shouted a challenge and McGirr turned towards the voice with the shotgun in his hands. The Det operator was armed with an HK53, a cut-down version of an assault rifle that looked and handled like a heavier-calibre variant of the venerable MP5 submachine gun made famous by the SAS during the Iranian Embassy siege. The HK53 was fast-firing and particularly lethal at close range. McGirr was hit thirteen times by two bursts, killing him almost instantly.

Meanwhile, on hearing the Det operator's challenge, Campbell began to run towards the car. Several other operators broke cover to chase him. As the sound of the gunshots that felled McGirr rang out, Campbell stopped and began to turn back towards his pursuers. The operators all opened fire together as they manoeuvred forward, discharging some thirty rounds at their target. Firing on the move is not conducive to a good aim and every shot missed. The Det operator who had taken down McGirr now turned his attention to Campbell. He fired two aimed shots from a stationary position, both of which missed, and then two more. Having escaped the first thirty-two rounds fired at him, Campbell's luck finally ran out and the last two hit home. He crumpled to the ground.

With Campbell out of action, two of the operators opened fire on the driver of the brown Talbot, hitting him. Despite his wounds, the driver sped away from the scene. A cut-off group in a nearby field opened up on the car as it passed, hitting it several times, but the vehicle dashed through their field of fire and the driver managed to make good his escape.

Back in the field, the Det operators who moved forward to secure Campbell's weapon found that he was still alive. One of the men, trained in emergency first aid, applied a shell dressing to his wounds in an attempt to stem the flow of blood. When Campbell began to have difficulty breathing, the medic carried out an emergency tracheotomy and inserted a plastic tube into his throat to bypass the blocked airway. His efforts were ultimately unsuccessful. Campbell died in the medic's arms five minutes after he was shot.

Campbell and McGirr both received full PIRA paramilitary funerals, including a volley of shots fired over their coffins by a masked 'honour guard'. The Armalite rifle that was recovered from the scene was forensically tested and linked to four murders of off-duty members of the security forces. The shotgun had been stolen by armed and masked men from a nearby farmhouse.

Since the late 1970s, the PIRA had increasingly turned its attention towards attacks on off-duty and often part-time members of the locally-recruited Ulster Defence Regiment and Royal Ulster Constabulary. These were the softest of targets, often assassinated while they were at their most vulnerable: at home, at their places of work or even attending church. These assassinations had the effect of driving more members of the loyalist community into the arms of Protestant paramilitary groups and poured more fuel on the fire of the vicious sectarian conflict. The assassination of an off-duty UDR man in a border area led almost inevitably to the killing of an innocent Catholic in retaliation by Protestant terrorist groups.

These killings also had a direct effect on the morale and conduct of regular security force personnel. This was especially the case with the mainly Protestant UDR and RUC, who were often prone to 'overreact' in the periods immediately following the murder of their own. Heavy-handed policing had its own knock-on effects, undermining efforts to foster better relations between communities and serving as a valuable recruitment tool for the republican terrorist organisations. Due to the direct and indirect effects of these assassinations, in 1983 all TCGs were tasked to do their utmost to prevent these killings. The operation in Dungannon that resulted in the deaths of Campbell and McGirr was part of this effort.

In February 1984, Londonderry Det received intelligence from Mid-Ulster TCG about a PIRA ASU operating in the staunchly republican area of Dunloy, North Antrim. The Det launched a surveillance operation with the objective of interdicting any attempts to target off-duty members of the UDR and RUC. The particular target of the surveillance was a PIRA volunteer named Henry Hogan, a die-hard republican from a staunchly Nationalist family (another member of the family was serving a twelve-year prison sentence in Portlaoise Prison in the Republic of Ireland at the time of the operation).

Intelligence suggested that Hogan was a member of an ASU that was responsible for a number of recent attacks and that he was actively planning to carry out another in the immediate future. In the week prior to the shootings of Campbell and McGirr, Det operators attempted mobile surveillance of Hogan and other suspected members of the ASU. However, they were thwarted by the effective anti-surveillance tactics employed by Hogan, who successfully identified a Det car that was following him in the Draperstown area.

Given the immediacy of the threat, and despite the fact that Hogan was aware he was under direct surveillance, it was decided to insert a covert OP to watch Hogan's house. Given the risks involved, the Det turned the mission over to one of their most experienced and skilled operators, Sergeant Paul Oram.

The OP was inserted at night. Oram and another operator approached the Hogan house across a field, shielded from view by a group of huts used by local workmen. The huts also provided cover for the OP site itself, located some eighty metres from the target. However, due to constraints imposed by limited time and Hogan's anti-surveillance measures, the Det operators were unable to carry out a preliminary survey of the proposed site. Unbeknown to them, light from a nearby street lamp reflected directly onto the position they intended to use and cast a long shadow onto the field behind them. This shadow instantly betrayed the movements of the operators as they established the OP.

Hogan, already on the alert, spotted the shadows moving in the nearby field and quickly called together an ASU comprising himself, a PIRA volunteer named Declan Martin and a third man who was never identified. Hogan armed himself with a Vigneron 9mm submachine gun, a post-war Belgian weapon that bore a striking resemblance to the famous Nazi-era MP40. Martin carried an Armalite rifle and the third PIRA man was armed with a double-barrelled shotgun. Other PIRA members were assigned to carry out a diversion, with the goal of keeping the attention of those in the OP fixed on the events in front of them.

The diversion team arrived in a blue Mini just before 8 p.m. and began to mill about in the street while a man in dark clothing came from the rear of the Hogan house and moved towards the vehicle. With the distraction in place, Hogan's ASU left the building by the back door, dressed in combat clothing and balaclavas. They manoeuvred out of sight through the streets, working their way round to enter the field behind the unsuspecting Det operators. The ASU then approached the OP from the rear with their weapons cocked and ready. As they neared the position, Hogan called out to the two operators to stand up and put their hands in the air. Any sudden moves, he warned, and he would blow their heads off.

This was the stuff of nightmares for any Special Forces soldier serving in Northern Ireland. The Det team had been taken unawares and was now outnumbered and outgunned by PIRA terrorists in a superior tactical position. But neither operator considered laying down their weapons for even a moment. Both men knew that surrender would mean inevitable torture and death. That left only one possible response.

Oram's companion moved first. He turned to face the approaching enemy with his Browning 9mm drawn and fired off a shot at Martin, hitting him badly enough to prevent the PIRA man from shooting back. Oram, armed with an MP5 'Kurz', spun his weapon round and opened fire at Hogan, causing a minor injury. Hogan responded with a burst from his Vigneron, then took off across the field with Martin, the pair apparently deciding that men who shot back were not the sort of targets they were comfortable facing. The third PIRA terrorist did not engage at all, instead opting to flee the scene as soon as the shooting began. His shotgun was later found abandoned in a nearby field.

The damage, however, was already done. Hogan's single burst had hit both of the operators. Paul Oram was killed instantly. The second operator, although badly wounded, managed to make an emergency call for assistance on his personal radio. An immediate reaction team in an unmarked civilian car arrived within minutes to secure the area. One of the team spotted the wounded Hogan and Martin trying to make good their escape. He shouted at them to stop and drop their weapons. When they did not, he fired at both terrorists, knocking them to the ground. With the threat neutralised, the operator rushed back to administer first aid to the men in the OP.

Another member of the reaction team approached the downed PIRA men to secure their weapons and check for signs of life. As he did so, one of the men on the ground moved and, believing he was about to be shot, the operator fired twice into the prone body. Hogan and Martin were both pronounced dead at the scene.

Forensic tests carried out on the weapons recovered at Dunloy revealed that the Armalite rifle carried by Declan Martin had been used in the murder of a policeman four months earlier. Constable John McFadden was shot dead outside his home in Rasharkin while off duty.

Paul Oram was coming towards the end of his second tour with 14 Intelligence Company when he was killed in action. A man of humour and modesty, his stock answer when asked what he was doing in Northern Ireland was, 'I'm doing a job for Maggie', referring to then Prime Minister Margaret Thatcher. The death of this professional, fearless and dedicated soldier was felt as a personal blow by everyone who had had the privilege of meeting him, including the author of this book.

The continuing efforts of the TCGs to interdict attempts at killing off-duty security personnel increased in the wake of the Dunloy shootings. In December 1984, Londonderry Det received a tip-off from a highly-placed source inside the PIRA of an imminent attack. An off-duty part-time member of the UDR had been targeted for assassination at his place of work, the Gransha Psychiatric Hospital. This information was unusually specific, naming the two PIRA terrorists who would carry out the attack as Daniel Doherty and William Fleming. The source indicated that the two men intended to carry out a 'dummy run' on or about 6 December, while the actual killing was planned to take place the following day.

Daniel Doherty was a committed and dedicated terrorist who had joined the junior branch of the PIRA (Fianna Éireann) when he was just fourteen. By the age of twenty-three, he had a considerable history of terrorist activity behind him. Doherty had already served a four-year sentence in Portlaoise Prison in the Republic of Ireland for IRA membership and possession of explosives. He was also believed to be responsible for the assassinations of a number of off-duty security force personnel, including the shooting of another UDR man at the same hospital in 1980.

William Fleming, aged nineteen, was the brother of Kieran Fleming, the PIRA man who had drowned while extracting from the ambush in County Fermanagh that resulted in the death of SAS Corporal Alistair Slater. Intelligence reports indicated that he too had been involved in a number of attacks on security force targets.

Londonderry Det launched a surveillance operation against Doherty and Fleming. The overall operational plan was for the Det to track the pair while they carried out their 'dummy run'. An SAS strike team would then be deployed at the hospital the next day to await the actual assassination attempt. Londonderry Det was tasked with following Doherty and Fleming up to the moment they moved into the hospital grounds, at which point they were to pull back and leave the waiting SAS team to do their work. In the event, things did not go exactly to plan.

On the morning of 6 December, Doherty and Fleming, both wearing crash helmets, rode towards Gransha Hospital on a motorcycle, shadowed by several Det cars. A number of other Det operators were in the area of the hospital on foot. As dawn was breaking, just before 7.45 a.m., the operation started to go awry. Instead of driving past, as expected, the motorcycle drove straight onto the hospital grounds. The Det operator in the vehicle immediately behind the motorcycle realised that this was no dummy run and that the assassination of the off-duty UDR man was about to take place. He made the immediate decision to intervene and rammed the bike, starting a contact that shattered the early-morning calm of the hospital grounds.

The collision knocked Fleming, the pillion passenger, off the bike, but Doherty somehow managed to maintain his balance and turned the motorcycle around in a desperate attempt to escape. The Det operator stopped his vehicle and exited the car with his weapon drawn. Fleming, who was armed with a pistol, was shot three times. Det operators quickly closed in on the area, appearing from the surrounding streets to try to cut off Doherty's escape. The next moments were pure chaos.

Seeing his route blocked, Doherty drove his motorcycle straight towards one of the cut-off team. The operator fired at both Doherty and Fleming with his 9mm Browning pistol, letting loose a total of eleven shots before running out of ammunition. He then deployed his primary weapon, an HK53, and fired more rounds at each of the terrorists, unaware that Fleming had already been put out of action.

A second Det operator who had arrived on foot engaged at the same time, firing at both terrorists with an MP5 submachine gun. Doherty, who had been hit a number of times, steered wild and ran his bike into a kerb. The collision knocked him to the ground, where he was shot a further six times. In total, the three Det operators fired fifty-nine rounds, hitting Doherty nine-teen times and Fleming four. Both Doherty and Fleming were pronounced dead at the scene.

John Hume, an SDLP Member of Parliament, called for an emergency Government statement concerning the incident but his request was denied. The killing of two terrorists who had come armed to murder a man in a hospital caused an outcry in some republican circles. The claim that the Army had followed a 'shoot to kill policy' was made loudly and often.

As always, the truth is not straightforward. None of the Det operators who went out on 6 December 1984 did so with the inten-tion of killing Doherty and Fleming. The core role of 14 Intelligence Company was surveillance, not the interdiction of terrorists. That job belonged to the SAS. However, when faced with faulty intelli-gence and the realisation that an innocent off-duty UDR man was about to be killed, the operators were forced to react to a dangerous situation as it evolved. While the firing of so many rounds may seem excessive, the operators on the ground needed to make snap decisions in the heat of combat against two armed terrorists bent on murder. It is not surprising that they acted in the manner in which they did. It also has to be remembered that, ultimately, the operators' actions saved at least one innocent man's life.

Although PIRA ASUs increasingly focused their attention on soft targets, the best propaganda to support the claim that they were fighting a war against occupying forces came from engaging security force units in the field. In January 1985, an RUC source informed his handler that the PIRA unit in the border town of Strabane was planning an ambush on an RUC police car. The attack was to have two components. First, newly developed hand-held launchers would be used to fire armour-piercing grenades at the vehicle. Then, as any surviving police officers exited the wreck, they would be shot by a heavily-armed fire team using automatic weapons. The potential for a massacre, with heavy security force casualties, was classed as 'imminent' and 'critical'.

The source could not, or would not, specify when the attack was to take place. As a result, intensive surveillance of the Strabane area was carried out in an attempt to locate the ASU, but to no avail. Given the immediacy of the threat, the RUC handler took the unusual and risky step of contacting his source again. This time he was given the location of a possible arms dump that might be used by the attackers, located in a field about half a mile outside the town.

On the night of 22 February, a team of three Det operators deployed an OP to the area where the weapons cache was thought to be located. This was a high sloping field next to the Plumbridge road, surrounded by thick hawthorn and crested at the top by a hedge. The OP team, carrying HK53 rifles with the standard

9mm Browning pistol as backup, settled in to wait in cover at the bottom of the field while other operators took up support positions nearby. The team hoped to locate the arms dump before the PIRA ASU could use the weapons stored there to launch an attack. What they didn't know was that the weapons were already gone. The PIRA unit had launched its operation.

In the early hours of 23 February 1985, a five-man PIRA ASU set off to carry out mass murder. The team consisted of Charles Breslin, aged twenty, brothers Michael Devine and David Devine, aged twenty-two and sixteen, respectively, Declan Crossan, aged twenty-two, and another, unknown, terrorist. The ASU had previously scouted the scene of the intended attack and identified a routine that they could exploit, noting that an RUC patrol car passed the spot regularly at about 4 a.m. each morning. The ambush was set, with two terrorists each carrying a shoulder-launched grenade launcher and an armour-piercing grenade. The three other men carried a range of automatic rifles: a .223 FNC; a .223 Ruger; and a heavier but more powerful 7.62 FN FAL, similar to the British Army's standard rifle of the time but with a fully-automatic capability.

Fortunately, thanks to a timely warning from RUC Special Branch, all police patrols had been ordered to alter their normal movement patterns. As a result, the ASU's intended target did not turn up at the appointed time. After a short wait, the PIRA men decided to abort the ambush. Crossan and the unknown member of the team handed their weapons over and departed for home, leaving Breslin and the Devine brothers to return to the arms dump with the intention of concealing the rifles and launchers for use another day.

The three Det operators all had their eyes fixed forward, watching for any sign of movement near the area where the as yet unidentified arms dump was supposed to be located. The approach of the remainder of the PIRA ASU from a completely different direction nearly caught them by surprise. Hearing footsteps, the operators turned to find three heavily-armed men walking towards them from the direction of nearby Springhill Park. What happened next was an immediate contact.

The PIRA team had been wearing balaclavas for their ambush of the RUC patrol car but had pulled these up when the mission was aborted. Now, seeing movement ahead of them in the dark, the terrorists pulled the balaclavas down over their faces again and swung their weapons towards the new threat.

This brief delay was fatal. Unlike in the incident at Dunloy that cost Paul Oram his life, the Det operators in the OP had sufficient time to react and opened fire first. In total, the three men fired 117 rounds at their targets as they closed in on the ASU using a classic fire-and-manoeuvre contact drill. Each man moved forward towards the enemy in short bounds of two or three steps while the others provided covering fire. Two of the operators drew their trusty Browning 9mm pistols as they closed, unwilling to lose the momentum of the attack when their rifles either jammed or ran out of ammunition.

A street light in the nearby Head of the Town housing estate cast its light towards the scene of the contact as the operators advanced. One of the men in the support group knocked it out with two bursts of automatic fire, fearing that it would illuminate the OP team as they manoeuvred towards the enemy. The lessons of Dunloy had been well learned.

By the time the reaction teams arrived a few minutes later, the contact was over. They discovered Charles Breslin, Michael Devine and David Devine all dead from multiple gunshot wounds. Declan Crossan was later identified from forensic evidence and sentenced to twenty years in prison for conspiracy to murder for his part in the attempted ambush. The fifth PIRA terrorist was never identified.

The weapons recovered were forensically tested. All were found to be loaded and all had rounds in the breach. The .223 Ruger rifle had been used in the murder of an off-duty part-time UDR man, Robert Gregory Elliot, at Castlederg, on 2 January 1984. He was shot fourteen times at close range by two gunmen as he got into his van to go to work. Elliot died on the ground outside the home he shared with his widowed 69-year-old mother.

Eight months after the failed ambush, on 7 October 1985, the PIRA shot a young man by the name of Damien McCrory, putting two bullets in the back of his head and leaving his body by the roadside. Damien was twenty years of age and had severe learning difficulties. The PIRA claimed that he had 'confessed' to working for the RUC for thirteen months and that he had 'set up' the three terrorists who died outside Strabane. RUC Special Branch has no record of Damien McCrory ever working as an informer.

The first half of the decade had been an eventful time for 14 Intelligence Company, with successes that were hard-won and losses keenly felt. Thanks to the professionalism and unselfish efforts of its operators, many innocent lives had been saved and many potential terrorist outrages prevented. Recognition of the vital role played by the three Det units in containing the terrorist threat in the Province was reflected in the formation of a completely new detachment, 9 Det, in the second half of the decade. Like the operations of its predecessors, 9 Det's actions would lead to yet more inaccurate accusations of a British 'shoot to kill' policy in Ulster.

CHAPTER EIGHT

THE ENEMY

There were only two banned republican terrorist organisations when widespread violence broke out in Northern Ireland in 1969: the IRA and, the relatively unknown, Saor Éire (Free Ireland). In the years to follow, the republican movement would undergo repeated splits and changes in leadership due to political disputes, arguments about strategy and personal differences. These changes led to the creation of dozens of different terrorist groups of various sizes and capabilities, and also to the complete overturning of the established dominance of the IRA itself. Ultimately, the crushing of internal dissent and the forging of a largely unified republican policy was to be one of the decisive factors in bringing the Troubles to an end.

Saor Éire

Saor Éire was formed in 1967. Viewing themselves as Marxist guerrillas dedicated to the overthrow of imperialism and capitalism, members of the organisation considered politicians and political institutions both north and south of the border to be equally legitimate targets. Most of Saor Éire's armed actions were carried out in the south of Ireland and the group's 1971 manifesto is striking in that it spends far more time attacking the government of the Republic than it does the British. Predictably, given the political views of the vast majority of Irish and British citizens, the group was completely ineffectual in their goal of launching a Marxist revolution and their activities never advanced beyond bank robberies and the occasional shooting or bombing aimed at escalating political tensions. The organisation ultimately disbanded in 1975 after the shooting of one of its key leaders.

While Saor Éire played no significant role in the Troubles themselves, the circumstances behind their formation in 1967 were, in many ways, a taste of things to come. The kernel around which the organisation was formed was a group of disenchanted former members of the IRA who had left in dismay at the organisation's lack of military activity. Just two years later, similar tensions over the IRA's dwindling appetite for violence led to a much more dramatic split that tore the old organisation apart.

The IRA

By 1969, the Irish Republican Army was a very different organisation to that which had led the struggle for Irish Independence in the war of 1921. In the nearly half a century that had passed since that defining success, what had once been a mainstream organisation with broad popular support had become a fringe group relegated to the margins of Irish politics. The hardline members of the IRA rejected the treaty that had formed the basis for peace between Britain and Ireland, not only condemning British rule in the north but also rejecting the legitimacy of the Irish state in the south as well. For the true believers of the organisation, the government in the south of the island were sell-outs and it was the IRA Army Council alone that constituted the true and lawful government of the island. For decades, a key part of the identity of the IRA remained the refusal of its members to take part in the official politics of either Britain or the Irish state, a policy that was to lead to frequent splits in the organisation whenever a faction began to take steps down the road to peace.

So committed were the IRA to the long-term fight against the British that, during the Second World War, the organisation's leaders went so far as to collaborate with the Nazi regime in Germany. In exchange for German support in their struggle, IRA leaders proposed a German invasion of Northern Ireland that would be supported by republican land forces. Unsurprisingly, there were few in either the north or the south of the island who sympathised with such extreme measures.

In the immediate aftermath of the allied victory, with only a few hundred active members remaining and very limited supplies of arms, the IRA had little ability to continue its conflict with Britain. It was not until 1957, after a long period of rebuilding, that it was again in a position to launch a sustained military campaign. The strategy chosen by the IRA's leadership was to carry out attacks on British military and government infrastructure in border areas, using 'flying columns' based in the Republic of Ireland. The goal was to make large areas of the country ungovernable and to demonstrate that British control could not be maintained in the face of armed opposition. The 'border campaign', as it became known, was a disaster. Only a handful of British security force members lost their lives over the five years of the campaign, while eight IRA men were killed and hundreds more arrested. Worst of all, the campaign received almost no popular support in Northern Ireland.

With the strategy of direct military confrontation completely discredited for the time being, the leadership of the IRA increasingly fell into the hands of men, such as Cathal Goulding, whose political sympathies lay with the radical left. Throughout the 1960s, a socialist ideology began to replace the old sectarian nationalism that had previously been the core motivating force of the organisation. With it came a tendency to minimise the specifically Catholic identity of the IRA and to see the organisation as representing all the working-class peoples of Northern Ireland. This shift in mindset led to the IRA running down its military establishment and focusing instead on its new radical socialist agenda. A military campaign against the British would only serve to intensify the divisions within the Irish working class, the movement's intellectuals argued, while the primary goal of the IRA should now be to bring them together. 'Revolutionary struggle' became the organisation's new goal. Physical force was seen by the leadership as a counter-productive tactic, even if not as wholly illegitimate.

The IRA, like the governments of Britain and the Republic of Ireland, was completely unprepared for the outbreak of inter-communal violence in 1969. The move away from sectarianism made it reluctant to play its traditional role of defending Catholic neighbourhoods from Protestant violence and of carrying out reprisals against the Protestant community. In the wake of the widespread civil disorder sweeping through the province, the IRA's leaders gathered together in Dublin to debate the overturning of the longstanding policy of abstentionism. By a three-to-one margin, those present agreed to recognise both the British and Irish governments and for members who were elected to parliament to take their seats. While this progressive move had the potential to help calm sectarian tensions, to many of the more traditionalist republicans it seemed like a betrayal of everything the IRA was meant to stand for. The organisation immediately split, with the traditionalists forming the new Provisional IRA (PIRA), while the rump of the old organisation became known as the Official IRA (OIRA).

The Official IRA and the INLA

The Official IRA terrorist campaign in Northern Ireland was, at best, half-hearted. Unwilling to carry out the sectarian killing of civilians, and with an ideology that saw violence against Britain as counterproductive, the OIRA's scope for action was initially limited to the defence of nationalist neighbourhoods and the protection of arms caches. These limitations did not, however, completely remove the potential for conflict.

The policy of protecting arms caches led to a major clash with the British Army in July 1970, when soldiers entered the Lower Falls area of Belfast to search a street for weapons that the OIRA had deployed in response to loyalist attacks. The British troops quickly discovered fifteen pistols and a large amount of ammunition, as well as a number of other weapons. As the soldiers prepared to leave, they were confronted by angry crowds of stone-throwing locals. The British troops responded with CS gas and the situation quickly deteriorated into mass disorder. Local residents barricaded streets, denying access to the security forces, while British officers ordered more and more men into the area in an attempt to suppress the resistance. Eventually, the British commander on the ground imposed a curfew in the hopes of clearing the streets. The tactic was unsuccessful and by the end of the night clashes with OIRA units had begun, leading to three soldiers being shot and wounded.

Believing that the Army intended to carry out further searches, and unwilling to give up the arms located in the area, Jim Sullivan, the OIRA commander in the Falls, decided to fight the British for control of the streets. Over the next two days, between sixty and one hundred OIRA gunmen fought running battles with security force units in the largest sustained combat engagement of the Troubles. By the time the Army had re-established control over the streets, four civilians were dead, hundreds of rounds of ammunition had been fired and over a thousand houses had been searched.

In operational terms, the Battle of the Falls was a significant success for the British, with the OIRA forces driven off and over one hundred firearms captured. But from a strategic perspective it was a disaster. Turning a nationalist neighbourhood into a warzone in order to remove weapons intended for self-defence against vicious sectarian attacks did catastrophic damage to the idea that the Army had been deployed to Northern Ireland to protect the Catholic community from loyalist violence. The Falls Curfew marked a decisive and irreparable breach in the relationship between the British Army and Northern Irish Catholics and began a downward spiral that soon turned to open and enduring hostility. Many young Catholics flocked into the arms of both the OIRA and the PIRA as a result.

The OIRA continued to carry out what it considered to be defensive operations. Despite declaring a ceasefire in May 1972, sporadic attacks on members of the security forces continued whenever the organisation's leadership felt retaliation was warranted. Seven British soldiers were killed over the next year. However, as time passed, the OIRA became increasingly focused on achieving its aims by peaceful means. In 1974, this led to a second split. Seamus Costello, a senior officer and one of the movement's more left-wing thinkers, quit the OIRA to form the Irish National Liberation Army (INLA), a fanatically militant revolutionary socialist organisation.

The OIRA's manpower and resources were now more frequently expended in feuds with its splinter groups, the PIRA and INLA, than with the British. The conflict with the INLA led to the deaths of senior members on both sides, including Billy McMillen, the veteran OIRA Belfast Brigade commander, and, in

1977, Seamus Costello himself. With most of its militant members having left to join the PIRA or the INLA, and with a long-term ceasefire in place, the Official IRA faded from significance. While still existing as an organisation, by the late eighties the security forces no longer considered the OIRA to be a threat.

The INLA continued to operate throughout the seventies and into the eighties from its strongholds in Londonderry and the Divis Flats area of Belfast. It gained a reputation during this time as a small but lethal terrorist organisation. Among its most notable operations was the successful assassination in March 1979 of the Conservative MP Airey Neave, Shadow Secretary of State for Northern Ireland, using a car bomb planted in the car park at the House of Commons. The INLA described the bombing as 'the operation of the decade'. The single worst atrocity carried out by the organisation occurred on 6 December 1982, when a disco at the Droppin Well bar in Ballykelly was bombed without warning. Eleven soldiers and six civilians were killed in the attack.

The INLA continued to be an effective threat to the security services throughout the Troubles. However, their operational capability was greatly diminished from the mid-eighties onwards after testimony given by 'supergrass' Harry Kirkpartick led to the conviction of twenty-seven members. While most of these convictions were soon overturned, the distrust that was sown by the well-placed informer, and the increasing fear of betrayal, led to further splits within the group. Disaffected members splintered to form the Irish People's Liberation Organisation

(IPLO) in 1986, and for the next six years much of the INLA's energy and resources were expended in a fruitless feud with their former associates.

The Provisional IRA

From the very beginning of its existence, the Provisional IRA was Catholic to the core, conservative and very, very violent. The organisation under its first Chief of Staff, Seán Mac Stíofáin, was wedded to the belief that a united Ireland could only be achieved through physical force. This core ideology of violence was given a gloss of democratic legitimacy by Sinn Féin, the political arm of the movement, which had rejected its leaders' moves to end abstentionism and switched its loyalties wholesale from the OIRA to the PIRA.

Between its formation, in 1969, and early 1971, three catastrophic events in Northern Ireland – the Falls Road Curfew, Bloody Sunday and the introduction by the British government of internment without trial – resulted in PIRA membership soaring. Disaffected young Catholic men and women flocked to its ranks as the most visible and active symbol of republican resistance to both loyalist violence and the British state. While the majority of its recruits came from the youth of Northern Ireland, the PIRA was initially funded by prominent political figures in the Republic. It later received money from a variety of sources, including protection rackets, bank robberies and smuggling, as well as large donations from wealthy Irish-American individuals and organisations.

In its early years, the PIRA operated under a quasi-military command structure built around units described as brigades, battalions and companies. For example, Belfast Brigade had three battalions: the 1st Battalion operated out of the Andersonstown, Lenadoon and Suffolk areas of the city; the 2nd Battalion was based in the Falls and Ballymurphy areas; and the 3rd Battalion covered North Belfast's Ardoyne and New Lodge Road areas. Battalions were then subdivided into companies, with each company having a number of Active Service Units (ASUs). Outside Belfast, brigades operated at the city or county levels, with some counties, such as Tyrone and Armagh, being divided further into regional brigades. While this organisational structure would persist throughout the Troubles, from the mid-seventies onwards, operational activities were carried out by ASUs acting largely as independent cells, to reduce the threat of successful British surveillance operations.

Command of the PIRA in Northern Ireland was in the hands of Northern Command under the control of a 'Northern Commander'. In the mid-seventies, Northern Command expanded to take in the border counties of the Republic of Ireland as well, where many attacks were planned and based. Southern Command continued to operate in the remainder of the south and was primarily responsible for the provision of logistical and financial support. Overall control of the PIRA rested in the hands of an eight-man Army Council, which included the Chiefs of Staff and leading representatives of both Northern and Southern Commands, as well as senior figures in Sinn Féin.

The PIRA's first concerted military campaign, carried out between 1971 and 1973, was extremely brutal, with 1972 being the bloodiest year of the entire conflict for both civilians and security force personnel. Even at this early stage, two figures were already emerging within the PIRA who were ultimately to rise to lead the organisation: Gerry Adams in Belfast and Martin McGuinness in Londonderry.

According to intelligence reports, McGuinness had personally killed at least eight members of the security forces and was one of the rising stars of the Derry Brigade in the early 1970s. Briefing reports on Adams indicated that he had been responsible for shooting one soldier dead and wounding another in his early career. His career as a senior figure in the movement began when he was appointed commander of the PIRA's 2nd Battalion in Belfast and then later briefly took on the role of brigade commander.

In his early years, Adams looked for guidance to two leading hardline IRA veterans, Brendan Hughes and Ivor Bell. Bell had taken part in the disastrous 1956–62 border campaign and then left the movement in disgust following its decision to call a cease-fire. Bell joined the newly-formed Provisional IRA in 1970 and became commander of B Company in Belfast's 2nd Battalion. He later served as Adams's deputy before becoming brigade commander in his own right and, ultimately, PIRA Chief of Staff. Hughes was another Belfast stalwart who rose through the ranks at the same time as Adams, taking on the role of brigade commander after Bell's capture. In 1972, Hughes had been responsible for the Bloody Friday bombings, which saw 20 bombs detonated across

Belfast in less than 90 minutes, killing 9 people, including 5 civilians, and wounding more than 100 others, including 77 women and children.

It was through the influence of hardliners such as Bell and Hughes that the PIRA developed its 'long war' strategy in the mid-1970s. During the first years of the Troubles, IRA leaders had believed that a mass armed rising across Northern Ireland could make the province impossible to govern and force Britain to withdraw through a swift military victory. As the momentum began to drain from this campaign in the years following 1973, the high command turned instead to the idea of the 'long war', a campaign designed to grind down over many years Britain's resolve to stay in Northern Ireland.

Not everyone in the organisation believed that such an approach could work. By the late 1970s, both Adams and McGuinness had determined that a military victory against the British was no longer possible, in no small part due to the increased efficiency of the covert operations that now constrained the PIRA's ability to mount operations. Abandoning the idea of sweeping the 'foreign oppressors' out of Ireland by destroying Britain's ability or will to rule, they formed a new strategy that placed a much greater emphasis on the political wing of the movement. Famously described as 'the Armalite and ballot box strategy', this new approach involved moving the PIRA towards becoming a legitimate political force. Ironically, part of the new strategy involved abandoning some of the elements of abstentionism that the PIRA had mobilised to support when they first formed in 1969.

By the early 1980s, the Adams/McGuinness faction had achieved a dominant position within the organisation and were able to make their policies the official position of the PIRA and Sinn Féin. They were not without their opponents, however. In 1984, Ivor Bell, who had lost his position as Chief of Staff following a period of imprisonment, openly opposed Adams's proposal. Bell immediately received strong support from other leading hardliners and it seemed as if a new split in the organisation was a real possibility. Adams moved swiftly to undercut the attempted rebellion. In June 1985, Bell was dismissed from the Provisional IRA, with the threat that if he joined any other republican movement, he would be assassinated.

As a result of Bell's expulsion, the Adams/McGuinness faction maintained firm control of the organisation in the critical urban areas of Belfast, Londonderry, Armagh and Newry. However, in the rural areas of East Tyrone and Fermanagh, there was an open rebellion against Adams's strategy. The leaders of the opposition to the new strategy were three figures who attained an iconic status within the movement: Jim Lynagh, Padraig McKearney and Seamus McElwaine.

Jim Lynagh was in his late twenties when Ivor Bell was expelled. A native of the Republic and one of twelve children, Lynagh joined the PIRA in his teens and served with the East Tyrone Brigade. He was badly injured in 1973, when a bomb his unit was working with exploded prematurely, and spent the next five years imprisoned in the Maze. On his release, he stood as a Sinn Féin candidate in a council election in his hometown of

Monaghan and began to gain a reputation as a political figure. At the same time, he immediately rejoined the East Tyrone Brigade and quickly rose through its ranks to become a leading figure.

Lynagh was strongly suspected of leading the PIRA unit responsible for the murder of Sir Norman Stronge, a retired senior member of the Ulster Unionist Party (UUP), and his son James, an RUC reservist and former British Army officer. The two men were killed at their home at Tynan Abbey, on 21 January 1981, when a heavily-armed PIRA ASU of at least eight men stormed the building. James Stronge managed to put up a flare to alert the security forces to the attack before he and his father were shot. The PIRA unit then destroyed the Stronge family home using incendiary devices. As they left the Stronge estate, the PIRA gunmen ran into units of the security forces and a fierce gun battle ensued. Despite the opposition, the ASU was able to successfully disengage with no casualties and melted away into the night.

This operation was characteristic of the approach advocated by Lynagh. During his time in prison, Lynagh had become a close student of the writings of Mao Tse-Tung and, subsequently, as he gained influence in East Tyrone, he advanced a strategy drawing on Maoist principles of guerrilla warfare. Lynagh believed that large flying columns of well-armed and disciplined PIRA men could take the war to the British, launching attacks on military installations near the border and denying the security forces control of the area. By creating zones that were free of British control, the PIRA could then establish its own directly ruled power base from which it could expand, mirroring the gradual spread of the communist revolution in China.

In 1984, Lynagh began to work with his long-time friend Paidraig McKearney, who shared his views concerning how the war should evolve. McKearney was born into a family with a long history of support for the Irish republican cause. He had joined the PIRA in the dark days of the early 1970s and was arrested on operations several times in the years that followed. In 1973, McKearney was convicted of possession of a firearm and sentenced to seven years in prison. Three years after his release on parole, he was again caught in possession of a firearm and sentenced to a further fourteen years in prison. After serving some three years of his second sentence, McKearney, along with Seamus McElwaine and thirty-six other republican prisoners, took part in a mass escape from the Maze Prison on 25 September 1983. Half of the escapees were recaptured in the following days but both McKearney and McElwaine made it to safety. McKearney immediately rejoined the East Tyrone Brigade.

In December 1985, the East Tyrone Brigade began to put into action elements of the plans that Lynagh and McKearney had developed. While the Army Council were unwilling to sanction a fully independent flying column operating from a permanent state of readiness deep in the rural areas of the border, the brigade was given permission to carry out attacks on RUC and Army bases. The first operation in this new phase of the terrorist campaign was carried out against an RUC station in Ballygawley in December 1985.

Lynagh's men struck the station under cover of darkness on the evening of 7 December. The officers on guard duty at the time – Constables George Gilliland and William Clements – were shot dead as they opened the gate to an apparently innocent visitor. Gunmen then stormed the building armed with assault rifles, sending the remaining RUC officers inside fleeing from a back door. The PIRA men searched the building for anything of value, planted a bomb and then withdrew. Once they had reached a safe distance, the bomb was detonated and the RUC station completely destroyed. Lynagh's men escaped without sustaining the slightest injury for their troubles. The victory was complete. Over the next two weeks, the East Tyrone Brigade carried out further demonstrations of their effectiveness with two mortar attacks on RUC bases, the second of which destroyed the station in Castlederg and injured seven people.

The next major operation staged by Lynagh's column took place in August of the following year. The target this time was an unmanned RUC station in the small village of The Birches in northern Armagh. While the security forces were distracted by a diversionary attack some fifteen miles away, Lynagh's team used a mechanical digger carrying a bomb in its bucket to first smash through the fence surrounding the station and then destroy the station with the resulting blast.

In late 1986 or early 1987, Lynagh and McKearney met at the home of Seamus McElwaine with a handful of other leading republicans who objected to the direction in which the Adams/McGuinness faction were taking the PIRA. Lynagh and McKearney were able to point towards the clear success of their operations against British bases and to argue convincingly that if their hands were not tied by the Army Council then they could be even more effective. Together with the others present, they discussed the possibility of striking out from the PIRA and acquiring their own sources of weaponry with the goal of putting Lynagh's strategy into full effect.

If the most active volunteers in the border areas around Tyrone had come together, possibly under Jim Lynagh's leadership, to pursue their own war against the British, the results would have been devastating for the strategy developed by Gerry Adams and Martin McGuinness. In 1986, the East Tyrone Brigade of the PIRA was the most significant threat faced by British forces in Ulster. The focus of the undercover war now turned towards infiltrating, disrupting and interdicting its operations. In this, the security services were aided by a stream of high-grade intelligence on the brigade's activities. The source of this intelligence was a senior member of the PIRA, close to, if not actually part of, the eight-man Army Council.

CHAPTER NINE

THE TYRONE BRIGADE

THE SAS (1985–90 – I)

The five years between 1985 and 1990 were among the most dramatic for the SAS during the entire undercover war. In this period of intensive operations, the East Tyrone Brigade of the PIRA was savaged and many of the most virulent opponents of what came to be known as the 'Peace Process' were eliminated. During this time the SAS saw many of its greatest successes and also some of its most controversial actions.

On Monday, 9 December 1985, fifty-seven shots were fired at Castledawson RUC Station in County Londonderry. No one was injured in the attack but the sheer weight of fire led to 14 Intelligence Company being tasked to carry out surveillance against the PIRA ASU operating in the area to determine how much of a threat they posed. The Det operators assigned to the task reported back that the ASU was badly organised and loose in their security procedures but still represented a serious risk to security forces in the area.

Two months later, an RUC source informed his handler that a pair of rifles had been dumped by members of the ASU in response to security force activity in the area. The weapons had been dropped hurriedly in a field behind a farmhouse east of Castledawson. According to the source, no effort had been made to conceal the rifles and the ASU intended to recover them later the same day.

Londonderry TCG immediately tasked a unit of Det operators to confirm the presence and exact location of the rifles. At the same time, two four-man SAS teams were assembled. The first team, wearing full uniform and carrying Armalites, moved into the target area at about 9.30 p.m. On arriving, they made their way swiftly and silently to the back of the farmhouse to stake out the weapons. The second team, in civilian cars and wearing civilian clothes, was deployed nearby to serve as backup.

The night was cold and clear, with a good moon and a well-lit, ground-floor window in the farmhouse helping with visibility. Not long after the primary SAS team had moved into position, the commander of the unit watched as a vehicle drove up and came to a halt near the building. Two men exited the vehicle, the first, a young man wearing a bomber jacket, followed moments later by a more elderly gentleman, slightly stooped and wearing a formal single-breasted jacket.

The two men were visibly nervous, their heads turning sharply from side to side as they peered into the shadows around the farmhouse, looking for any signs of suspicious activity. When they were satisfied that it was safe to proceed, the older man gave a signal that sent his younger associate off through a gap in the hedge to carry out a visual check of the field and the area in which the weapons had been dropped. After a brief look around, followed by a short, quiet conversation with his colleague, the younger man made his way back into the field again and moved directly to the location in which the weapons had been left. The SAS team commander watched as the man bent down, then straightened up, holding a rifle in one of his hands.

The sight of the firearm was exactly what the SAS commander had been waiting for. He quickly broke cover to intercept the gunman, advancing with his weapon ready in his shoulder and calling out loudly for the man to halt. The gunman spun towards the sound, both hands now on the rifle. The team leader and a second SAS man immediately opened fire and the gunman dropped to the floor. Unsure whether the target had been shot or had taken cover, the pair manoeuvred towards him, taking it in turns to provide covering fire for each other as they sprinted forward in short bounds. When they reached the gunman, they found that he was already dead. The second suspect took advantage of the chaos of the brief contact to make good his escape.

The dead man was Francis Bradley. Bradley, twenty years old at the time of the shooting, had first come to the attention of the security forces during a violent confrontation with RUC officers at the funeral of PIRA Volunteer Antoine Mac Giolla Bhrighde (shot dead by the SAS near Kesh in 1984). In the aftermath of the attack on Castledawson RUC station, Bradley had been named by an RUC source as a member of the ASU responsible and questioned by police officers. In the absence of any corroborating evidence to tie him to the events, he was released without charge.

A postmortem examination found that Bradley had been hit by a total of eight rounds. Before travelling to the arms dump, Bradley had purchased a pair of rubber gloves from a local shop and was wearing them when shot. Two rifles – an FNC and an Armalite – were recovered from the scene of the ambush; forensic evidence showed that both had been used in the attack on the RUC station. The Armalite had also been used in the murder of four members of the security forces and was tied to a further twenty attempted murders.

Colm Walsh (46), the owner of the farmhouse, and Barney McLarnon (56), the driver of the car, were arrested at the scene. Neither was convicted of any offence in relation to the incident and neither they, nor Bradley himself, could be conclusively linked to any terrorist organisation. Local sources later indicated that Bradley had been pressurised by the local PIRA unit into picking up the dumped weapons, calling into question the report of the RUC source who had previously named him as an active PIRA member.

As in all SAS shootings, the inquest raised questions about the version of events told by the soldiers involved. Forensic evidence presented at the inquest showed that at least some of Bradley's wounds were sustained from rounds that entered

Above: A Det operator sat well back from the window of his observation post while using early video surveillance equipment.

Below: A Det observation post, equipped with a long-lens camera.

Inset right: Watching the streets. The view from an elevated observation post onto a suspect location.

Above: An operator emerging from an observation post in the cellar of a house.

Below left: Captain Robert Nairac. In 1977, Nairac was abducted from a pub while pretending to be a republican operative, driven across the border, and murdered by a PIRA unit. His body has never been found.

Below right: A target under surveillance on the streets of Northern Ireland in the mid-1980s.

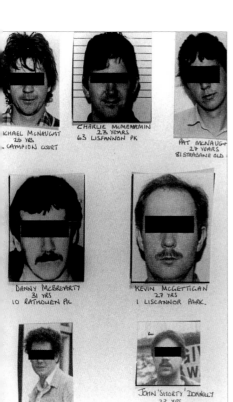

Left: Mugshots of suspects. Note the bottom two photos, which were taken by covert surveillance teams.

Above right: The PIRA's sniper campaign in the 'Bandit Country' of South Armagh proved to be one of the hardest threats to counter for British security forces. It was only in the closing days of the conflict that the SAS and the Det were able to mount an operation to capture one of the notorious sniper teams.

© *Liam Galligan / WikiCommons*

Right: A large improvised bomb discovered by members of the security forces in the late 1970s.

Left: Bernadette McAliskey (née Devlin), a republican activist. A constant target for loyalist terrorists, in 1981 she was shot nine times in her home. An SAS team watching her house gave McAliskey life-saving medical attention. In the aftermath, she nevertheless claimed that the British government had arranged for her to be killed.

Above: Derry (or Londonderry to the Unionists) was a nationalist stronghold throughout the troubles and the sight of the most violent urban unrest outside Belfast.

Below: Loyalist graffiti taunting the PIRA for their losses in the SAS ambush at Loughall.

Above: Gerry Adams led Sinn Féin for 35 years from 1983 to 2018. Along with Martin McGuinness, he was responsible for leading the PIRA into peace negotiations with the UK and, eventually, to the signing of the Good Friday Agreement and the laying down of the organisation's arms. Pictured here at Downing Street in 1999 – the site of an IRA mortar attack eight years previously.

© *Fiona Hanson / PA Images*

Left: The Downing Street mortar attack in 1991. Smoke billows from a burning van in Whitehall, London, 15 yards from a room where Prime Minister John Major was meeting with his cabinet. No one was injured.

© *PA Images*

Left: Soldiers, slogans and street barricades were the common backdrop to operations in the Province.

© *PA Images*

Right: Masked youths pelting members of the security forces with stones from behind hastily-erected barricades in Londonderry. 1981.

© *PA Images*

Left: Burnt out vehicles litter the streets of the Falls Road area in Belfast – the aftermath of the violence that erupted following the news that IRA hunger strike MP Bobby Sands had died. © *PA Images*

Right: Angelo Fusco was part of the 'M60 Gang' responsible for the killing of SAS Captain Herbert Westmacott. After escaping from British custody, he fled south to the Republic of Ireland, until 2000, when his case was dropped following the Good Friday Agreement.

© *Ógra Sinn Féin / WikiCommons*

Above left: The claim that 'There can never be peace in Ireland until the foreign, oppressive British presence is removed' was fundamental to the PIRA's identity in the early years of the Troubles. © *WikiCommons*

Right: A PIRA memorial to the three volunteers killed in Gibraltar while planning to detonate a car bomb. The funeral of Farrell, McCann and Savage was the scene of further violence when loyalist terrorist Michael Stone attacked the crowd of mourners, killing three and injuring more than sixty.

© *František Piliar / WikiCommons*

Left: Two boys walk past a wall with the painted slogan 'Twenty years on and still killing our children' on Ballymoney Street in Belfast.

© *Tony Harris / PA Images*

Top: 14 Int operators training with the HK MP5 'Kurz'. The Kurz replaced the MAC-10 as their preferred undercover weapon due to its accuracy and rate of fire. The small size had some disadvantages; the guard in front of the trigger was added after an SAS trooper accidentally placed his finger in front of the barrel while firing during the Iranian Embassy Siege in 1980.

Middle left: The Ingram MAC-10, the preferred car weapon of Det operators through the seventies and eighties, although SAS instructors derided it as 'a very expensive way of turning 9mm rounds into empty cases'.

Middle right: The Browning 9mm served as the workhorse pistol of Britain's Special Forces until 1998. Operators fitted extended 20-round magazines and often customised their weapons with larger safety catches to ensure they could respond to threats quickly.   © *US Bureau of Alcohol, Tobacco, Firearms and Explosives / WikiCommons*

Below: The AR-18 rifle, popularly known as the 'Armalite', was used on both sides of the undercover war, and became an emblem of the conflict in Northern Ireland.

© *WikiCommons*

through his back, either when he was facing away from the soldier who shot him or when he was lying on the ground. Predictably, these wounds led to claims that he had either been executed or shot unnecessarily as part of the supposed 'shoot to kill' policy. However, post-incident forensic analyses of this sort are unable to account for the chaotic reality of the life-and-death situations in which SAS and Det operators found themselves when faced with an armed threat. Bradley had retrieved a weapon and he had that weapon in his hands when shot. The soldiers involved can hardly have been expected either to wait for the suspect to complete his turn towards them or to cease firing as they advanced on a prone, but possibly still threatening, figure. Given the hard lessons learned in previous contacts, once a gunman was identified as a potential threat, SAS soldiers acted in a way that minimised the danger to themselves.

On the night of 23 April 1986, members of the Fermanagh Brigade of the PIRA placed a 357kg bomb, made from homemade explosives packed into ten creamery cans, into a culvert in the Rosslea area of County Fermanagh. A command wire was run from the culvert to a firing point, with the intention of detonating the hidden bomb at a later time as an army patrol passed by. The unit responsible for placing the explosives then withdrew.

The next day, an army foot patrol passing through the fields above the culvert noticed the badly concealed command wire. Rather than stop to examine the site and risk letting any PIRA observation post know that it had been discovered, the patrol commander told his men to keep walking. Once he was at a safe distance from the area, he radioed the location of the find in to headquarters, who then passed the information up to the TCG.

Later that day, the SAS were tasked to move to the Rosslea area, locate the command wire and establish if a culvert bomb had indeed been planted. A four-man SAS patrol was deployed to carry out the search in the early hours of 25 April. Searching for a bomb in the dark with the very real possibility that a PIRA gun team was already waiting in ambush was one of the most hazardous missions an SAS team could be deployed to tackle in Northern Ireland. Every man involved was familiar with the tragic events that had resulted in the death of Corporal Al Slater under similar circumstances eighteen months earlier. And every man knew that a single mistake, or even a piece of bad luck, could be enough to see them share his fate.

With the aid of the diligent reporting of the Army foot patrol, the SAS team leader quickly located the command wire and traced it back towards a hedgerow. The team closed in on the position in silence, taking care not to expose themselves to the likely field of fire of any ambushing unit. As the men inched closer to the target location, not knowing if they were in the gun-sights of a PIRA unit in a prepared defensive position, the tension rose to almost unbearable levels. The discovery that the location was vacant was met with audible exhalations of relief. The PIRA unit had chosen the position with great care. The hedgerow was ideally placed to serve as a firing point, with a commanding view of the road below and a ditch alongside to provide cover.

The SAS team split into two groups. Two men, one armed with a Heckler & Koch .223 rifle and the other with an Armalite, remained at the firing point. The SAS commander and another soldier, both armed with Armalites, moved to an observation position approximately 100 metres away, from where they could cover the likely approach. By the time everyone was in position, the day's first light was creeping up over the horizon.

The team settled down to wait. Each man remained concealed throughout the day, moving only to eat cold rations or to go through the unpleasant motions of relieving himself while maintaining his position. As night fell, and with no sign of the enemy, the team commander roused his men from their hides to examine the area in more detail, looking for locations that might give them a clearer view of the target or better cover from which to observe it. Unable to find a superior position, but grateful for the chance to stretch their cramped legs, the troopers returned to their initial hides to resume the long, uncomfortable wait.

Shortly before dawn on 26 April, at about 4.30 a.m., two armed men were spotted approaching the firing point. Both were wearing combat clothing and carrying rifles, later found to be a Ruger .223 and an FNC .223. The gunman armed with the FNC emerged from the cover of a ditch and was immediately challenged by the nearest trooper. As he turned towards the noise, the SAS man armed with the Heckler & Koch opened fire with a controlled burst.

One of the bullets struck the terrorist's rifle, sending up sparks that, in the darkness, were mistaken for shots being returned.

Both members of the SAS team now opened up on the target, then switched their fire to the second gunman, who dropped to the ground. Screams of pain could be heard from the direction where the second terrorist had disappeared from sight but neither of the SAS men were able to pinpoint his exact location in the gloom, despite launching flares to illuminate the area.

As the dawn light brightened, the SAS team took stock of the situation. One of the terrorists lay dead and two rifles were visible on the ground. Despite being badly wounded, the second gunman, Sean Lynch, had managed to stagger away to conceal himself in a nearby hedgerow, where he was discovered later that morning during a follow-up search. Despite his serious injuries, he was treated at the scene and survived to stand trial. Lynch was found guilty of possession of explosives and possession of a firearm, receiving a sentence of twenty-five years in prison. He was released in October 1998 under the terms of the Good Friday Agreement (GFA), having served a little under half of his sentence. After his release from prison, Lynch became active in politics as a member of Sinn Féin. In 2011, he was elected to the Northern Ireland Legislative Assembly (NILA) as the representative for Fermanagh and South Tyrone.

The dead PIRA man was Seamus McElwaine. McElwaine had already encountered the SAS once before, when his ASU surrendered after being surrounded in a farmhouse (see Chapter Six). Since his escape from the Maze Prison in 1983, McElwaine had been one of the most active leaders in the Fermanagh PIRA. Claims made by Sean Lynch that McElwaine was captured and interrogated before being executed by the SAS team are comprehensively denied by the soldiers involved, most of whom were decorated for their part in the operation.

McElwaine's death was celebrated in loyalist circles throughout Fermanagh and beyond. Within the security forces, his removal from the IRA's active service roster was seen as a major success. McElwaine was viewed as a highly skilled and dangerous terrorist, both hardened to the difficulties of the conflict and unrelenting in his desire to carry it through to the last.

The death of such a renowned killer at the hands of the SAS was a hefty blow to the prestige of the PIRA. McElwaine's prominence within the republican movement was on display at his funeral in the Republic of Ireland, which was attended by more than 3,000 mourners and watched over by 150 Gardaí in full riot gear. A volley of shots was fired over his coffin by a PIRA honour guard. Despite the ceremonial acts of remembrance, it can only be speculated what the PIRA leadership truly thought of his death. McElwaine was a close ally of James Lynagh and had been involved in discussions about breaking away from the PIRA to form a new hardline organisation. Like Lynagh, McElwaine had no time for the nascent 'peace process' supported by the Adams/McGuinness faction in the PIRA; had he lived, he would surely have been one of their fiercest opponents.

In early May 1987, James Lynagh and his East Tyrone Brigade set out to complete a major flying-column attack as part of his military strategy to create 'liberated' areas in the border regions. The target of the attack was the RUC station at Loughgall, County Armagh. Loughgall was a small, quiet village of some 350 inhabitants, most of whom were Protestants. The RUC station in the village was normally manned by six full-time and part-time RUC officers. On 8 May 1987, James Lynagh and his unit set out to kill them all.

At least fourteen members of the East Tyrone Brigade were to be involved in the operation, with a team of eight heavily-armed men prepared to carry out the assault on the station and six more serving in a variety of support roles. Shortly before the attack, five members of the unit arrived at a farm near Moy in County Armagh belonging to local man Peter Mackle. When Mackle's wife and daughters pulled into the driveway in the family car, the PIRA terrorists ordered them from the vehicle and informed the terrified civilians that they were taking the car, a mechanical digger used on the farm and a quantity of diesel oil. Two members of the unit then drove away in the stolen car, while two remained at the farm to prevent the family from reporting the theft to the authorities. The fifth man drove the digger to a nearby explosives cache to prepare for the attack.

Just before 7 p.m., the PIRA assault team assembled. A 200lb bomb had been placed in the bucket of the mechanical digger, which was to be driven by Declan Arthurs. Arthurs had joined the PIRA at the age of sixteen and was regarded by the security forces as a high-ranking member of the East Tyrone Brigade. He was an experienced operator of agricultural machinery and had also driven the digger in the attack on Ballygawley RUC station.

Earlier in the day, two other members of the brigade had stolen a blue Toyota HiAce van from a business premises in Dungannon, concealing it for later use. This van now served as the transport vehicle for the main assault team. Lynagh's men were dressed in blue boiler suits to give them some semblance of a uniform and their faces were covered by balaclavas. They were also armed to the teeth. Between them, they carried six automatic rifles (three Heckler & Koch G3s and three FN rifles of varying calibre), an Italian Franchi SPAS combat shotgun and a Ruger Security-Six revolver. The pistol had been taken from the body of a dead RUC officer in the aftermath of Lynagh's earlier attack in Ballygawley.

The men assembled for the operation were what Tyrone PIRA called its 'A' Team. In addition to Lynagh, McKearney and Arthurs, the team also consisted of Patrick Kelly, Michael Anthony Gormley, Seamus Donnelly, Eugene Kelly and Gerard O'Callaghan. Patrick Kelly was the East Tyrone Brigade commander and a staunch supporter of Jim Lynagh's strategic vision. Born in the largely Protestant town of Carrickfergus in County Antrim, Kelly moved to Dungannon when he was sixteen years of age. He came from a family with both strong republican traditions and a historical willingness to break with official IRA policy. His uncle had split from the IRA in the 1950s to found Saor Uladh, a small but extremely militant terrorist organisation that was active in the Tyrone and Fermanagh areas in the years preceding the IRA's Border Campaign.

Kelly joined the PIRA in the early years of the Troubles, rising to take command of the East Tyrone Brigade in 1985.

The following year, he attended the PIRA Army Convention, at which the abandonment of the principle of abstentionism was discussed. Kelly was part of the vocal minority who voted against the plan put forward by Adams and McGuinness and became firmly committed to Jim Lynagh's plan to break away from the PIRA and set up a new, uncompromisingly militant, organisation.

The attack on the RUC station in Loughgall had been carefully planned. Two scout cars, each containing a pair of men, were to be deployed to warn the assault team by radio of any security forces units approaching from the front or rear. The firefight was to be initiated by Declan Arthurs, who would use the digger to smash a hole through the perimeter fence of the RUC compound, before lighting a forty-second fuse attached to the 200lb bomb in the vehicle's bucket.

Lynagh had learned lessons from his previous attacks, and from that on the Ballygawley RUC station in particular. There, RUC officers had escaped by running out of the back door of the main building to find cover before the station was destroyed. For the Loughgall operation, Lynagh had brought in additional men to cover the rear. This time, he meant for nobody to survive. Shortly after 7 p.m., the mechanical digger began its journey down the road towards the Loughgall RUC station, with the Toyota van following closely behind. The approaching terrorists did not know that the SAS were ready and waiting for them.

Several weeks before the planned date of the attack, a high-ranking member of the PIRA had contacted MI5 directly to inform them of the impending operation. When the source intelligence reached Mid Ulster TCG, its authenticity was initially doubted by RUC Special Branch, who had managed to turn a well-placed informer of their own within the Tyrone PIRA, Tony Gormley, and Gormley had made no mention of any planned attack on Loughgall. Despite this, the weight given to the MI5 source was such that the Mid Ulster Det was deployed to carry out surveillance on Lynagh's 'A' Team. For three weeks, they watched as he and his men prepared for the operation. The claims of the senior PIRA source were quickly vindicated.

By the eve of the attack, the Det operators had confirmed both the target and Lynagh's plan. Unwilling to take any risks against such a heavily-armed flying column, it was decided to interdict the assault using overwhelming force. More than twenty SAS men moved into the area to set up a classic ambush, supported by members of the RUC's HMSU. A main 'killing group' was deployed near the station, with cut-offs further out to prevent any attempt to escape. In addition to their normal rifles, the killing group was armed with a pair of heavy belt-fed machine-guns to add to the weight of fire at their disposal. Six soldiers were positioned inside the station itself. There were several reasons for this tactical decision. Men in the station would be in a position both to meet any attempt to storm the building and to provide an additional angle of fire on the attacking IRA force. Most importantly, by placing men inside, the ambush commander would be able to counter any later claims by Sinn Féin propagandists that Lynagh's attack had been a 'harmless' attempt to destroy an empty building.

The digger and the van containing the PIRA assault team reached the RUC station at 7.20 p.m. Declan Arthur started the assault by driving his heavy vehicle towards the station, with Tony Gormley and Gerard O'Callaghan riding on the sides to provide covering fire, if needed. Arthur crashed the digger through the fence to breach the outer defences of the station, then leaped up onto the 'bucket' and lit the fuse of the bomb before falling back. Thirty seconds later, all hell was let loose in the quiet, sleepy town of Loughgall.

Lynagh's men jumped from their van and began to rake the RUC station with automatic fire. The waiting SAS teams immediately responded from their concealed positions, opening up on the attackers with everything they had. Even the enormous explosion as the bomb detonated did nothing to lessen the intensity of the SAS fire. Tony Gormley managed to fire a burst from his rifle before he was killed. Gerard O'Callaghan got off a single round from his SPAS shotgun before a burst of automatic fire cut him down as well. The remaining terrorists were all shot dead before they could bring their weapons to bear on the ambush party.

While the ambush was underway, a car containing two men was spotted moving towards the ambush site. The men in the car, brothers Anthony and Oliver Hughes, were both wearing blue boiler suits just like those worn by the members of the PIRA assault team. One of the SAS cut-off groups opened fire on the vehicle, mistakenly believing that it was a PIRA scout car driving to the aid of the attackers. Anthony Hughes was killed and his brother Oliver wounded. Both were innocent men who happened to be in the wrong place at the wrong time.

With the exception of the tragic but understandable error that led to the shooting of the Hughes brothers, the ambush was a stunning success. The entire PIRA assault team had been eliminated while the only casualties sustained by the security forces were a number of lightly wounded men inside the RUC station who had been injured by the bomb blast. The SAS commander on the ground in Loughgall, a senior NCO, received the Distinguished Service Medal, one of the highest awards for gallantry that can be awarded in the British Army. A number of other members of the SAS teams present also received gallantry medals.

The weapons recovered in the attack were examined by RUC forensics experts and found to have been used in at least seven murders. Four UDR members – Thomas Irwin, Martin Blaney, George Shaw and William Graham – had been shot while off duty. Three civilians – John Kyle, Ken Johnstone and Harry Henry – had been murdered by the PIRA for the 'crime' of supplying building materials to the RUC.

Some have argued that the amount of force used by the SAS in engaging Lynagh's unit was disproportionate and represented another example of the supposed 'shoot to kill' policy. However, the plain facts of the matter belie such claims. Jim Lynagh and his unit unquestionably intended to carry out a mass murder in Loughgall that day. His men had a long history of perpetrating similar attacks and the forensic evidence collected from the weapons showed that they had been used to assassinate at least seven unarmed individuals. Lynagh's men initiated the firefight by shooting first and by detonating an enormous explosion, only then being engaged by the SAS. The fact that the SAS deployed large numbers and heavy weaponry to neutralise the threat in no way amounted to a disproportionate use of force. The goal was to win the firefight as quickly as possible and with as little risk as possible. Trying to achieve the same aim with a lower weight of fire would have achieved absolutely nothing.

Initial news reports about the ambush reported a major terrorist attack on Loughgall RUC station leading to 'multiple casualties'. Cheers rang out in the republican wing of Crumlin Road Gaol in Belfast, with the prisoners singing IRA songs and hanging Irish tricolours from the windows of cells. As more accurate reports began to seep out, the republican wing fell silent while the loyalists took their own turn to celebrate.

It soon became clear that the PIRA had suffered their single biggest loss since the beginning of the Troubles. Not since 1921, when twelve IRA men were killed in an ambush during the War of Independence, had casualties on such a scale been suffered by any republican militant group. In the wake of the news, there were sporadic outbursts of violence in Catholic areas of Lurgan, Portadown, Downpatrick, Coalisland, Strabane and Newry. The atmosphere in Protestant areas mirrored that on the loyalist wing of Crumlin Road Gaol, with near-universal jubilation. Some, though, had a more sombre perspective on the day's events. Ian Phoenix, a senior member of RUC Special Branch, wept at the 'waste of life'.

Despite the loss of so many of its best men, the Loughgall ambush did not immediately reduce the terrorist activities of the East Tyrone Brigade. In the two years prior to the ambush, the PIRA killed seven people in East Tyrone and North Armagh. In the two years following, they would kill eleven more and would launch several more major attacks against security force bases. In addition, the East Tyrone Brigade also carried out many of the terrorist attacks in the neighbouring county of Fermanagh during this period.

In time, however, the effects of the ambush made themselves felt. The men who died that day were the most experienced and hardened members of the brigade. Those that remained were, for the most part, younger, less experienced and less skilled. In the absence of Jim Lynagh and Patrick Kelly, the brigade now lacked dynamic and charismatic leadership with a sense of strategic vision and the power to convince others to follow that vision. Nevertheless, several men within their ranks tried to fill the void in the years that followed, with varying degrees of success.

An enduring mystery concerning the events in Loughgall is the identity of the PIRA source who informed MI5 about the operation several weeks in advance. The intelligence community considered the source to be sufficiently important that a cover story was leaked to the press claiming that the security services learned of the plans when they intercepted a telephone call between two of the terrorists involved. The true source of the information has never been revealed.

Several years before the ambush, the author of this book was enjoying several drinks with a serving MI5 officer when he heard a surprising claim. The author, young and ill-informed as he was at the time, was loudly opining that the best way to bring down the IRA would be to target its leadership, and to remove Gerry Adams in particular. The somewhat inebriated MI5 officer's response was surprising: '*No! He's one of ours!*' The author cannot confirm whether this claim was true or whether it had its origins in the kind of drunken bravado that leads to all sorts of tall tales in the mess. However, the look of shock on the officer's face immediately after the words came out, and his refusal to continue the conversation, were certainly suggestive, as was the fact that he was unwilling to ever speak with the author again in a non-formal setting.

It is interesting to note that a recently declassified letter in the Irish state archives claims that Adams was widely suspected of responsibility for the Loughgall attack in republican circles. Father Denis Faul, a Roman Catholic priest with close ties to the republican movement, wrote to the Irish government in 1987 with reports of 'intriguing' rumours in republican circles. According to his letter, certain members of the PIRA believed that Gerry Adams had set up the Loughgall ambush because Lynagh and McKearney had threatened to assassinate him due to their hostility towards his political strategy.

Whether or not there is any truth in the rumours about Gerry Adams is impossible to say with any confidence. What is certain, however, is that a very senior figure in the PIRA betrayed Lynagh and his companions. The deaths of Lynagh, McKearney and Patrick Kelly removed any suggestion that the East Tyrone Brigade might secede from the PIRA and start a new terrorist organisation. Over the coming years, the SAS, supplied by a stream of high-level intelligence from MI5, would further degrade the capabilities of the East Tyrone PIRA. It seems an unlikely coincidence that much of this intelligence just happened to be directed against figures in the PIRA who had the potential to threaten the leadership's path towards a negotiated settlement with Britain.

CHAPTER TEN

DEATH IN THE SUN

THE SAS (1985–90 – II)

Danny McCann was considered by the security services to be one of the deadliest close-quarter assassins ever produced by the PIRA's Belfast Brigade. In 1987, McCann was responsible for the murder of two RUC Special Branch officers as they drank in their local pub after work. McCann, together with fellow IRA member Séan Savage, walked calmly into the Liverpool Lounge near Belfast's passenger ferry terminal and gunned down Detective Constables Michael Malone and Ernest Carson at close range, injuring a third RUC man and a civilian as they made their escape. It was the kind of operation requiring nerves of steel and a single-minded focus on killing for which McCann was the perfect instrument.

McCann had a long history of terrorist involvement. Born in the Catholic Clonard district on the Lower Falls in Belfast, he first came to the attention of the security forces at the age of sixteen, when he was arrested for participating in a riot and sentenced to six months' imprisonment. As soon as he was released, McCann joined the PIRA. Six years later, in January 1979, he was caught in possession of a detonator and sentenced to two years in prison. Then, in May 1981, he was arrested again on suspicion of possessing a firearm but freed without charge.

But four months later, he – together with Savage and four other PIRA members – was arrested and charged with the murder of RUC Constable Alexander Beck.

Constable Beck had been driving an RUC Land Rover through the Suffolk area of West Belfast when his vehicle was destroyed in a rocket attack. His colleague, Michael Paterson, lost both his arms in the explosion but went on to overcome his injuries and become a highly respected clinical psychologist specialising in helping victims of trauma. The prosecution of McCann and his unit failed due to lack of evidence and all six men were released.

McCann had been a long-time supporter of the ousted PIRA leader Ivor Bell and was a vocal critic of the Adams/McGuinness strategy of seeking a negotiated settlement to the conflict in Northern Ireland. He even went so far as to quit the movement for a time in protest at the PIRA's moves towards peace. However, by 1987, he had rejoined the organisation and was determined to inflict heavy casualties on the security forces.

Despite being nearly ten years younger than McCann, Seán Savage was an equally dedicated proponent of 'physical force' republicanism. In addition to the terrorist attacks he had carried out alongside McCann, Savage was known to the security forces through source intelligence as the leader of his own PIRA

ASU. In December 1987, Savage's unit planted a car bomb in a vehicle belonging to John McMichael, one of the leading figures in the loyalist paramilitary Ulster Defence Association (UDA). McMichael survived the initial blast, despite losing both his legs, but died of his injuries in hospital shortly afterwards.

Mairéad Farrell was one of the relatively few female members of the PIRA to play a frontline role in the armed struggle in Northern Ireland. As with McCann and Savage, Farrell was dedicated to the use of terror in pursuit of her goal of a united Ireland and, in April 1976, a month after her nineteenth birthday, she was part of an ASU that attempted to bomb the Conway Hotel in Dunmurry, on the grounds that the hotel was sometimes used by British soldiers.

The attack went badly wrong. Farrell was arrested shortly after planting the bomb. Two other members of the unit, Sean McDermott and Kieran Doherty, broke into a nearby house, intending to steal the keys to a car parked outside. What the IRA men did not know was that the house belonged to a reserve RUC officer, who was at home at the time. When he was ordered to hand over his car keys, the policeman pretended to agree and reached into a cupboard. Instead of the keys, his hand came back out holding his service pistol, with which he promptly shot McDermott dead. Doherty fled the house but was arrested shortly afterwards.

Farrell was sentenced to fourteen years' imprisonment for her part in the operation. Doherty received eighteen years and died while on hunger strike in the Maze in 1981. Farrell survived her sentence, despite refusing food for a time, and was released in 1986. Soon after, she returned to active service with the PIRA.

McCann, Savage and Farrell shared a fierce commitment to their cause. All three had served significant prison sentences for their activities without turning informer or walking away from the movement. And all three had unflinching histories of violence that showed a willingness to inflict civilian casualties just as readily as to target members of the security forces. Together, in March 1988, they set out to commit mass murder in the British overseas territory of Gibraltar.

The target of the attack was to be the Changing of the Guard ceremony of the 1st Battalion, the Royal Anglian Regiment. The instrument of destruction: 141lbs of Semtex, 25 blocks of 2.55kg each, packed together into a lethal car bomb. Had the attack succeeded, the death toll among both military personnel and the civilians assembled to watch would have been appalling.

The Gibraltar attack had been authorised at the highest level of PIRA command. And just as quickly as it had been authorised, so it was compromised. Shortly after the attack had received the seal of approval from the PIRA's leadership, MI5 received detailed information about Danny McCann's role in the planned operation from a highly placed source within the organisation. Acting on this intelligence, the full resources of Britain's undercover security services were turned over to foiling the attack. The RUC's E4A, 14 Intelligence Company, MI5, MI6 and the anti-terrorist team of 22 SAS all played a role in the events that unfolded. The first step was an intensive surveillance operation targeting McCann.

For the next few months, McCann was shadowed across Belfast by a constant E4A presence. When he left to carry out his first reconnaissance mission in Spain, using a false passport in the name of Reilly, the reins were picked up by officers from MI6. In turn, MI6 received valuable help on the ground from Spanish intelligence, who cooperated fully throughout the entire operation. Spain's security services had been eager to help counter the threat, conscious as they were of the strong links between the PIRA and Eta, the Basque separatist group that was conducting its own campaign of terror against the Spanish government.

In mid-November 1987, McCann returned to Spain to continue his preparations. This time, he was accompanied by Savage and a female PIRA member using a stolen passport in the name of Mary Parkin (Parkin's real identity has never been revealed by the authorities). The group were again shadowed closely by MI6 and Spanish intelligence agents before flying back from Malaga to Dublin via Madrid.

The planned Gibraltar bombing had been blown from the very start, but, as if that were not enough to damn the operation, McCann himself also compromised the attack. In early February 1988, McCann met for a drink with Brendan Davison, the PIRA commander in the Markets area of Belfast. The pair knew each other well: Davison had been part of the unit arrested with McCann and Savage after the rocket attack that killed Constable Alexander Beck in 1981. During their conversation, McCann confided in Davison that he would be away for a while, as he was going to Spain for a 'recce'. What McCann didn't know was that Davison was a long-time RUC Special Branch informer. The information about McCann's planned reconnaissance mission in Spain was quickly passed on to his police handler. Some reports have claimed that Davison was already under suspicion by the PIRA's internal security unit. Whether or not this is true, he did not survive long enough to face an investigation by the feared 'nutting squad': in July 1988, Brendan Davison was shot dead by an assassination team from the Ulster Volunteer Force (UVF).

In February 1988, 'Parkin' flew to Valencia and then travelled south, followed by MI6 and Spanish intelligence officers, now augmented by a surveillance team from 14 Intelligence Company. Her destination this time was Estepona, a small town on the Costa del Sol, strategically situated between Gibraltar and Marbella. After checking in to the Buena Vista Hotel, Parkin began to carry out her own surveillance, all the while watched closely by her security service shadows. On 23 February, they observed her as she watched the Changing of the Guard in Gibraltar and then followed her when she returned to the Rock again on 1 March.

The activities of Parkin made it clear that the planned attack was coming closer. Back in Northern Ireland, the already heavy surveillance on McCann and Savage was intensified even further, with nearly all of the Det's Belfast operators being used for the task. At some point during the month of February, source intelligence informed MI5 that Mairéad Farrell was part of the PIRA team and would act as its leader. She, too, was put under intense observation.

At 2.15 p.m. on 3 March 1988, 14 Intelligence Company operators watched as Farrell left her home and drove towards the Irish border. MI6 operatives took over surveillance duties once she entered the Republic and followed her to Dublin airport, where she was seen boarding a plane for Brussels using the identity of one Mary Johnston. Another contingent of intelligence agents in Belgium watched as Farrell transferred to a flight to Malaga, this time switching to a passport in the name of Katherine Alison Smith.

On the same day, McCann and Savage travelled from Belfast to Dublin, watched first by members of E4A and the Belfast Det and then by MI6. The pair flew into Paris, where they stayed overnight, and then continued on to Malaga. On arriving in Malaga, McCann and Savage rendezvoused with Farrell outside the Banco Exterior at the airport. The three terrorists had been identified as they arrived in the country by agents belonging to the Spanish intelligence services. However, the team responsible for monitoring the arrivals lost contact first with Farrell and then with McCann and Savage when they hailed taxis to take them from the airport. As a result, the British intelligence services were in the dark for several frustrating hours about the movements of the PIRA attack team.

Eventually, Spanish agents coordinating with MI6 were able to trace the PIRA team to the Hotel Escandinavia in Torremolinos. McCann had booked into the hotel under the name of Edward McArdle, while Savage used the pseudonym of Brendan Coyne. Farrell arrived separately and spent the night in the same room as her accomplices.

The next day, Saturday, 5 March, Farrell left the hotel and joined up with a PIRA support team in order to acquire three vehicles for use in the operation. A red Ford Fiesta was rented from a car hire firm in Torremolinos by a man using the name of John Oakes and a white Renault 5 was acquired from an Avis outlet in the same town. The third car, a white Fiesta, was hired by Farrell from a Spanish rental company in Marbella.

During this period, British intelligence were relying entirely on their Spanish counterparts to continue the surveillance operation on the PIRA team. With limited resources available to them, it proved impossible for the Spanish security services to maintain a constant close watch over all members of the team, as they divided up and then came back together after carrying out different tasks. As a consequence, Farrell's acquisition of the white Ford Fiesta was not discovered until some days later and British intelligence laboured for a time under the misapprehension that only two vehicles were involved in the operation. This oversight was to have significant repercussions.

The next morning, Sunday, 6 March, a Spanish observation team picked up Séan Savage as he drove the white Renault 5 south along the coast road towards Gibraltar. The Spanish agents followed Savage as far as the border, where he was picked up by a British surveillance team. Savage then made his way through the congested traffic of the town to find a parking space. The position he selected was extremely close to where the 1st Battalion of the Royal Anglian Regiment were scheduled to perform the Changing of the Guard ceremony later that day. Any bomb detonated in that location would be sure to rip a bloody hole through the crowd, with dozens of guaranteed fatalities. Once his car was in position, Savage walked back across the border onto Spanish territory. There, he rejoined McCann and Farrell, who had driven south separately in the red Fiesta and parked on the Spanish side of the border.

With the team assembled, McCann, Savage and Farrell walked back into Gibraltar on foot. As they reached the border, their presence was picked up by officers from MI6 working alongside specially selected operators from 14 Intelligence Company. The British surveillance team followed the PIRA ASU as it made its way through the town again in the direction of the car that Savage had parked earlier. Also waiting on the Rock were over a dozen members of the 22 SAS Anti-Terrorist Team. The anti-terrorist role at the time was assigned to B Squadron and nearly half of the entire team had been deployed to Gibraltar to intercept McCann, Farrell and Savage.

Command of the SAS troops was technically in the hands of two officers, who were responsible for monitoring the overall situation and liaising with other services. However, the troops on the ground, the men who would actually intercept the terrorists if given the order, were led by a senior NCO. The man assigned this demanding task was a former Parachute Regiment soldier with a long SAS career behind him. He had served several tours in Northern Ireland with both the Paras and the SAS and had been part of the ill-fated Operation Mikado during the Falklands War, an attack on the Argentinian mainland that had gone badly wrong.

The NCO was no stranger to high-profile anti-terrorist work. As part of the team that had stormed the Iranian Embassy in London in 1980, he had gained some unusual insights into command priorities during anti-terrorist operations. While the attack on the embassy was still being planned, the NCO, a corporal at the time, had been assigned to drive a group of senior officers from the SAS, the police and the intelligence services to an area immediately outside the embassy building. During the journey, he listened in with interest as a discussion took place among the brass concerning the preferred option for resolving the crisis with the minimum loss of civilian life.

The senior SAS officer in the vehicle informed his colleagues that the current plan was to offer the terrorists a bus to take themselves and their hostages to the airport, from where they could fly out of the country. The bus would be driven by a disguised SAS volunteer, who would take the vehicle to a safe location where it could be stormed and the terrorists 'neutralised'. On listening to the plan, one of the senior police officers present observed with some concern that the driver of the bus would be in an extremely vulnerable position. The SAS officer nodded his agreement and replied that they would certainly have to 'write him off', but that the other saved lives would make the sacrifice worthwhile. None of the officers present realised that the humble corporal who was driving them to their destination had also volunteered to be the unwitting sacrificial lamb. Fortunately for him, the plan was changed before he could be sent to his death. Eight years later, the same NCO was in a position to steer a major operation himself as the commander on the ground for what had been designated

Operation Flavius. He was determined not to play with the lives of any of the men for whom he was responsible.

Following confirmation that Savage had parked his car in a position to attack the Changing of the Guard parade, a conference was organised by the British commanders. The meeting was overseen by Gibraltar's Commissioner of Police and other officials from the British and Gibraltarian governments. Also present at the meeting were the senior SAS officers on the Rock, members of the intelligence services and bomb disposal officers. Contrary to later reports, all present believed that Savage's car contained a powerful bomb designed to cause mass casualties and all now expected the PIRA ASU to return to launch the attack. As a result, when McCann, Savage and Farrell were observed crossing the border into Gibraltar again, everyone in a position of authority believed that they intended to detonate the bomb. It was also believed that, following normal PIRA practice, each of the attackers would most likely be armed.

The SAS does not act without both legal and political oversight and the steps that had to be taken before British troops could draw their weapons in a civilian environment were well-established. Before the SAS team on the ground could intercept the PIRA ASU, control of the situation had to be passed formally from civilian to military hands. Until confirmation of the handover was received, the SAS men would be unable to do anything other than follow and watch.

McCann, Savage and Farrell walked into Gibraltar town from the border, shadowed as they went by MI6 operators, two teams of

SAS soldiers and a number of police surveillance specialists. After about a mile, as they reached the junction of Winston Churchill Avenue and Smith Dorrien Avenue, Savage was seen to split from his two companions and began moving away from them. Civilian and police officials listening to reports from those on the ground came to the conclusion that Savage had noticed he was being tailed. Fearing that Farrell was about to 'arm' the bomb, they formally handed operational control over to the SAS.

The SAS officer in overall command took the radio and said clearly over the network, 'I have control.' These simple words informed everyone, and especially the SAS men on the ground, that the rules had changed: this was now a military operation in which soldiers were authorised to use lethal force. The next words out of the officer's mouth set that force in motion: 'Stand by … Stand by … Go!'

Hearing these words, the senior NCO moved to intercept McCann and Farrell, supported by another SAS man. The undercover soldiers drew their 9mm Brownings as they closed, believing that the terrorists were likely to be armed. At the same time, a second two-man team began to pursue Savage.

As the senior NCO moved in, McCann stepped forward to put himself between Farrell and the approaching SAS men. With their line of sight to Farrell blocked and McCann apparently shielding her, the two soldiers now had another reason to think that Farrell was about to arm the bomb. The NCO's eyes met those of McCann for the briefest of moments. Before the SAS man could shout a warning, McCann made an abrupt movement with his arm. Fearing that he was reaching for either a remote detonator or for a weapon, the SAS NCO opened fire, hitting McCann and dropping him to the floor. As the line of sight to Farrell opened up again, he saw her grab at the handbag under her arm. Unwilling to take the risk that she had the detonator, the NCO immediately fired again, bringing Farrell down, before turning his attention back to where McCann was still moving on the ground. Three more quick shots, including two to the head, ensured there would be no opportunity for McCann to pose any further risk. In the few seconds it took for the contact to resolve, the second member of the SAS team also opened fire, first on Farrell and then on McCann.

While the threat from McCann and Farrell was being neutralised, the second team were closing in on Savage. Hearing shots ring out behind him, Savage spun round quickly towards the noise. Despite being ordered to stop by the advancing soldiers, he made a sudden movement that both SAS men interpreted as reaching into his jacket. The two soldiers opened fire together, hitting Savage in the chest and head.

The contact had lasted only moments but ended with all three members of the PIRA ASU dead on the street. The aftermath of the events was to demonstrate the extent to which perceptions in the heat of the moment could be pre-shaped by expectations. When Savage's white Renault 5 was inspected by bomb disposal experts shortly after the shootings, it was found to be empty. McCann, Savage and Farrell had all, in fact, been unarmed and had not entered Gibraltar that day with the intention of carrying out their attack just yet. The bomb they planned to use had been transferred by the PIRA support team to the third hired vehicle, which was discovered by the Spanish police two days later, packed with Semtex and shrapnel in a car park in Marbella.

Much has been written and broadcast about the involvement of the SAS in Operation Flavius. A number of witnesses have come forward to dispute the SAS version of events and accusations have been made that the operation was a conspiracy between the SAS, British intelligence and the civilian authorities to assassinate the three PIRA terrorists who were killed in the incident. A jury at an inquest held in Gibraltar later that year concluded, on the basis of a 9–2 majority, that the shootings were justified. A later European Court ruling voted by 10–9 that the killings were not 'absolutely necessary', that the three PIRA terrorists *could* and *should* have been arrested at the border and that security forces involved had used excessive force; *however*, the same court unanimously cleared the British government, the SAS and the intelligence services of operating a 'shoot to kill' policy and rejected any claim for the payment of compensation to the families of the slain terrorists.

As with other claims concerning the operation of a 'shoot to kill' policy, the fact of the matter is that there was no conspiracy. Everyone involved simply believed, wrongly as it turned out after the events, that the three terrorists had planted a bomb and that they likely had the means to detonate it remotely. The members of the SAS teams responsible for intercepting McCann, Savage and Farrell knew that they faced highly dangerous, professional and dedicated terrorists who would not hesitate to kill them or to detonate a bomb to cover their escape. In the fractions of seconds in which the soldiers had to make decisions that could result in the loss of their own lives or those of innocent civilians, it is not surprising that they did not prioritise the well-being of known terrorists as more important. The potential risks the PIRA unit posed to life and limb were clear and that they intended to plant a bomb that would have caused a devastating loss of civilian life is unchallenged. In such circumstances, it is hard to blame the soldiers for the actions they took and harder still to shed tears for the three deceased, who had spent months plotting the large-scale slaughter of innocents.

A secondary, more tragic, consequence of the Gibraltar shootings was the spiral of violence that they set off in Belfast. The emotional ferment that followed Operation Flavius was to plunge the province into one of the darkest periods of its already tragic conflict.

A week after the shootings, on 14 March, the bodies of the three PIRA terrorists were flown on a charter aircraft to Dublin, where they were met by large crowds. The coffins were then driven north amidst a heavy security presence before being handed over to the families of the dead. British security forces were deployed in large numbers throughout Belfast in an attempt to prevent demonstrations. During the night, tensions were stoked further when Kevin McCracken, a PIRA member, was shot dead while preparing to ambush a security force patrol.

The funerals of McCann, Savage and Farrell were due to be held two days later at Milltown cemetery on the outskirts of

Belfast. In order to avoid further clashes, the RUC agreed with the families of the dead that the police would keep a low profile during the ceremony. On 16 March, taking advantage of the minimal security force presence, a loyalist terrorist by the name of Michael Stone attacked the mourners as they stood at the gravesides, throwing hand grenades and shooting into the crowd with a pistol. Thomas McErlean, John Murray and Kevin Brady were all killed in the atrocity and more than sixty others were wounded. Stone was chased and eventually knocked to the floor by the enraged crowd, only surviving thanks to the intervention of a mobile RUC patrol who placed him under arrest.

A second wave of funerals followed for the victims of Stone's murderous rampage. The atmosphere was fraught as the crowds gathered for each burial prepared to defend themselves in the event of any further loyalist attacks. The funeral of Kevin Brady, the only PIRA member among Stone's victims, was arranged for 19 March. As the procession made its way along Andersonstown Road in the southwest of Belfast, the crowd was alarmed when an unknown car cut across its path.

The vehicle, driven by two young British Army corporals, had no business being in the area at the time and it is not known why the men were anywhere near the procession. Seeing that the road behind them had been blocked off by vehicles, the corporals attempted to drive through the crowd ahead in order to escape. They quickly found themselves hemmed in on all sides by hostile mourners who suspected they were members of a loyalist group intent on further slaughter.

Furious at the idea of another attack, members of the crowd started to break their way into the vehicle to get at the men inside. One of the corporals responded by drawing his pistol and firing a single warning shot in an attempt to clear a path to escape. After drawing back for a moment, the crowd closed in again and dragged the two soldiers from the car. Both were disarmed and thrown down to the ground, where members of the crowd began to beat them. PIRA members soon arrived to take control of the situation. The wounded soldiers were placed in a taxi and driven away from the procession to a nearby area of waste ground. There, they were stripped of their clothes and subjected to further assaults before being shot repeatedly with a pistol that had been taken from their car.

The murder of the two soldiers was filmed by a British Army helicopter that was powerless to intervene in the savagery unfolding below. Those who have had the misfortune to see the video in its entirety are invariably haunted by the appalling scenes that it captures. Margaret Thatcher described the killings of Corporal David Howes and Corporal Derek Wood as the 'single most horrifying event' to take place in Northern Ireland during her time as Prime Minister. The author can only agree.

The criminal investigation into the killings ultimately led to the conviction of a number of those who had been involved. Harry Maguire and Alex Murphy were found guilty of the murders in 1989 and given life sentences. Both men were released under the terms of the Good Friday Agreement nine years later. Thirty-nine others were charged with lesser offences related to the killings.

Precisely why the two corporals were in the Andersonstown area on that fateful day will never be known. Both men were special forces signallers and had already visited various locations around Belfast before they encountered the PIRA funeral procession. Corporal Howe had been in Northern Ireland for just one week. The best guess (and it can only be a guess) is that Corporal Wood was taking his companion on a 'familiarisation tour' of the city when he got lost and accidentally drove into the path of the procession. Any suggestion that the two unfortunate men were on operational surveillance duties is totally misguided. Had the men been either 14 Intelligence Company operators or SAS personnel, they would undoubtedly have rammed or shot their way out of the situation, rather than firing a single warning shot over the crowd. One experienced SAS man, John McAleese, put it to me this way: 'They might have got me out of that car, but they would have had to climb over a lot of bodies to do it.'

Michael Stone, the UDA terrorist whose attack on the funeral in Milltown Cemetery had created the conditions for the corporals' killings, was convicted of the three graveside murders and another three sectarian killings to which he confessed under questioning. He was given sentences totalling 684 years but was released in 2000 under the terms of the Good Friday Agreement. Six years later, Stone was arrested while attempting to carry out an attack on the seat of Northern Ireland's devolved government at Stormont. Stone's defence lawyer claimed that the attack was not intended to harm anyone and was, in fact, 'a piece of performance art replicating a terrorist attack'. Unconvinced by this argument, the British government re-imposed the full sentence for his earlier conviction, to which a Belfast court added another sixteen years for his actions at Stormont. In 2013, the Court of Appeal added a further eighteen years to Stone's sentence for the Milltown Cemetery murders. After hearing of the judgment, a former RUC Special Branch officer declared to me with a wry smile that Stone 'had suffered for his art'.

CHAPTER ELEVEN

OPERATIONS

THE SAS (1985–90 – III)

Between 1985 and 1990, the PIRA became the most heavily-armed terrorist group in Europe. The main source of weapons for the organisation had traditionally been sympathisers in the United States. In the 1970s, the principal conduit for these weapons was George Harrison, an Irishman who had emigrated to New York as a young man before the Second World War. It is estimated that Harrison's operation was responsible for purchasing and smuggling over 2,500 guns, including significant quantities of the formidable Armalite AR-18 and AR-15 rifles.

In the late 1970s, the PIRA's US smuggling network was bolstered by the arrival of Gabriel Megahey. Megahey was able to develop contacts in the Boston underworld who assisted him in acquiring more Armalites and other modern weapons, including several belt-fed M60 machine-guns. The M60 had served as the workhorse fire-support tool for the US army during the Vietnam conflict and proved deadly in PIRA hands. One of the weapons smuggled across by Megahey was used to fight off an SAS attempt to storm a building in 1980, killing the team's leader, Captain Herbert Westmacott.

Both Harrison and Megahey were arrested in operations led by the US Federal Bureau of Investigation (FBI) in the early 1980s. Megahey was sentenced to seven years' imprisonment after being caught trying to buy anti-aircraft missiles on the black market. Harrison's trial was a rather less straightforward affair. Harrison's lawyer, Frank Durkan, pursued a highly unorthodox legal strategy that accepted that his client had indeed been a gun smuggler but argued that the smuggling had been approved by the US government. When the prosecuting counsel stated in court that Harrison had been smuggling guns during the six months prior to his arrest, Durkan objected on his client's behalf that the figure was an insult and that Harrison had been 'running guns for the last twenty-five years at least'. As the trial unfolded, Durkan managed to sow doubt in the jury's mind by arguing that the US Central Intelligence Agency (CIA) had approved the smuggling operation and that the agency's denial of this fact was simply to be expected from an organisation that operated in secret. The jury found this claim to be plausible enough to introduce reasonable doubt and Harrison was ultimately acquitted.

Durkan was a stalwart defender of supporters of the republican movement. In another case that spanned nearly a decade, he argued against the deportation to Britain of IRA gunman Joe Doherty. Doherty, a member of the M60 Gang responsible for the murder of Captain Westmacott, had escaped from prison in Northern Ireland during his trial in 1981 and fled to New York. With Durkan fighting tooth and nail on his behalf, it was not until 1992 that he was finally deported back to Northern Ireland to serve his sentence for murder. Doherty was ultimately released in 1998 under the terms of the Good Friday Agreement.

Despite the setbacks to the trans-Atlantic smuggling operation caused by the arrests of Harrison and Megahey, a steady flow of weaponry continued to find its way across the ocean. The scale of the ongoing operation became clear in 1984, when the Gardaí, acting on a tip-off from the FBI, intercepted a ship carrying over seven tons of arms off the coast of Ireland. The weapons were traced back to sources in the Irish Mob in Boston, where they had been acquired by the notorious Whitey Bulger's Winter Hill Gang. Increasing cooperation between US and British police and intelligence services continued to put pressure on PIRA smuggling operations and senior members of the IRA's leadership became concerned at the possibility that their main source of weapons might be choked off entirely.

These worries were swept away in the aftermath of the American bombing of Tripoli and Benghazi in Libya in 1986. Libya's revolutionary leader, Colonel Muammar Gaddafi, had been a long-term supporter of terrorist organisations who opposed the governments of the Western nations allied with the USA. Libya had provided arms to the PIRA on a sporadic basis throughout the seventies and early eighties, but after the American attacks in 1986, Colonel Gaddafi was determined to make Britain pay for allowing the US bombers to strike Libya from UK bases. In retaliation, he ordered the dispatch of three enormous shipments of weapons to the PIRA, totalling over 200 tonnes. These shipments included everything from flamethrowers to surface-to-air missiles and vast quantities of Semtex, as well as enough small arms and ammunition to equip a brigade of regular soldiers.

The third and largest of these shipments, amounting to more than 120 tonnes of weapons, was intercepted in November 1987 aboard the MV *Eksund* by ships of the French Navy operating in the Bay of Biscay. The first two shipments arrived safely, however, and the equipment they carried with them gave the PIRA access to military-grade arms and explosives far beyond anything that had ever been available to them before. No other European terrorist organisation could boast an armoury that came close to approaching that of the PIRA in terms of either quantity or sophistication.

The rearming of the PIRA was a major setback for the British forces involved in the undercover war. SAS soldiers and Det operators knew that the terrorists they faced would be more heavily-armed than ever before. AK-47s, RPG 7 rocket launchers and Soviet DShK heavy machine-guns now became standard issue items for most PIRA units.

* * *

On 1 July 1988, a PIRA ASU from the Ardoyne area of North Belfast mounted an attack on the RUC station at North Queen Street. Special Branch had been tipped off about the impending operation in advance by a well-placed informer in the north

Belfast PIRA and the SAS were tasked by Belfast TCG to intercept the ASU. The SAS team assigned to the operation was led by an experienced sergeant, John McAleese.

John McAleese – or John Mac as he was known in the regiment – had been watched by millions across the world in 1980 as he and another SAS man set the frame charge on the balcony of the Iranian Embassy in London that began the assault on the building. He had served many tours in Northern Ireland since joining the SAS in 1975 and was decorated for gallantry for his actions in the province. During his seventeen-year career in the SAS, John Mac became one of its most recognisable figures and was known by all as an outstanding soldier.

Despite his military virtues, the feature that excited the greatest comment among John Mac's fellows was his uniquely peculiar legs, which had strange bony protrusions jutting out at the knees. During the build-up to Operation Mikado, a planned raid by B Squadron on Argentinian airfields during the Falklands War, John Mac and a number of other SAS personnel had walked into an RAF mess in search of refreshments. As John Mac put his foot up on a bar rail, the bony outcropping near his knee accidentally came into contact with a neighbouring drinker, giving the unfortunate airman a painful but temporary 'dead leg'. The sight of the man doubled over in sudden pain after nothing more than a nudge was enough to clear the bar. The rest of the RAF personnel present, the troopers later learned, had jumped to the conclusion that the poor fellow was the victim of deadly SAS martial artistry. Deciding that discretion was the better part of valour, the airmen had fled before the first unprovoked attack could turn into a more generalised outbreak of Special Forces violence.

The source intelligence John Mac received about the impending attack in North Queen Street suggested that the PIRA unit would carry out a drive-by shooting from a stolen car. The plan was to launch an RPG rocket at the front guard post of the police station and then spray the area with automatic fire from an AK-47 before fleeing the scene. John Mac's plan was to surprise the attackers by replacing the normal RUC personnel in the guard post with two SAS men, supported by a few select RUC personnel. A back-up team of four SAS men, including himself, would wait inside the police station, ready to respond instantly to events as they unfolded. In order to facilitate a swift exit from the heavily-fortified building, it was decided that the reinforced and armoured front gates would be left slightly open. A lever in the guard post could then be pulled to open the gates the rest of the way, allowing the four-man reaction team to dash out of the building and deal with the attackers, covered by the two SAS men in position in the guard post.

On the night of the attack, a hooded and armed PIRA team entered the home of an innocent Catholic family in the republican New Lodge area. The terrified family were held hostage at gunpoint while their car, a Volvo, was stolen. Just after midnight, the stolen Volvo, now containing three terrorists, approached the North Queen Street RUC station. As the car came to a halt across the road from the guard house, one of the men in the vehicle emerged from its sunroof armed with an RPG rocket launcher and fired a rocket at the guard house. The deafening sound of the impact was heard by RUC officers manning posts many streets away while the flash of the explosion lit up the night. Despite all the sound and fury, the rocket failed to penetrate the guard post, leaving only cosmetic damage on the concrete walls outside. As soon as the rocket exploded, a second terrorist raked the front of the building with a sustained burst of automatic fire.

The two SAS men in the guard house immediately returned fire, hitting one of the terrorists and laying down a controlled suppressing fire to cover the arrival of the reaction team. John Mac's men rushed to the front gate, ready to pour out into the street and engage the vehicle, but in the adrenaline-filled seconds after the explosion, the RUC man tasked with opening the gates pulled the wrong lever. The gates swung shut with a clang, trapping the reaction team inside the building for the few moments it took the PIRA unit to make their escape.

The two SAS men in the guard house continued to engage the terrorists as they exited their vehicle and fled. The PIRA team had brought a large duffel bag of clothes with them on the operation to allow them to change their appearance and blend in with the civilian population while escaping. As they scrambled from the car, the duffel bag slid off the back seat and rolled into the road. In the darkness, the SAS men in the guard post mistook it for a terrorist and fired at it. When the reaction team emerged from the station a few moments later, they also made the bag their first target.

Tragically, at almost the same time as the terrorists fired their first shots at the police station, a taxi driven by a Protestant named

Kenneth Stronge was passing along the road. Stronge was hit three times during the exchange of fire and critically wounded. He died in hospital three days later from a heart attack.

In the follow-up operation, RUC officers recovered an RPG rocket launcher, an AK-47 assault rifle, a mask and a bloodstained jacket from in and around the stolen Volvo. The identity of the wounded PIRA terrorist was never discovered. The North Queen Street shooting caused a great deal of friction between the SAS and the RUC, with both organisations blaming each other for the outcome. If there was any lesson to be learned from the episode, it was that even the best-laid plans can, in the heat of the moment, be derailed by the careless action of a single person.

John Mac would later be awarded the Military Medal for actions in Northern Ireland. Ten years after the North Queen Street operation, his son Paul followed him into the Army, something that filled John with pride. Paul rose to the rank of sergeant in the 2nd Battalion of The Rifles and proved himself to be an excellent soldier, just like his father. On 22 August 2009, Paul was killed in a bomb attack in Afghanistan as his patrol sought to recover the body of another British soldier. John Mac never really recovered from his son's death and died of a heart attack in Greece on 26 August 2011. Many of those who knew him believed that the real cause of death was a broken heart.

Barely a year after Loughgall, at about 12.30 a.m. on 20 August 1988, the East Tyrone Brigade of the PIRA made it clear that, despite their losses, they were still a force to be reckoned with. Members of the brigade mounted a major attack in Ballygawley,

County Tyrone, with the aim of disrupting British troop movements in the area. The target of the operation was a bus carrying thirty-two members of the Light Infantry regiment who were returning to active duty in Northern Ireland after a period of leave in England. The weapon of choice was a large bomb containing some 200lbs of Semtex, packed into a car parked by the side of the road from Ballygawley to Omagh.

As the bus passed the parked vehicle, a PIRA member detonated the bomb remotely by command wire from a firing position 300 metres away. The effect of the explosion was devastating. The ferocious blast stripped the metal sides and windows from the vehicle and propelled the exposed frame 30 metres down the road. As the skeleton of the bus hurtled wildly towards its final resting place, the dead and wounded soldiers within were flung out to land in the hedges and fields along the roadside. Eight soldiers were killed in the attack, all under the age of twenty-one, and many more were badly injured. The Semtex used in the attack is believed to have been provided to the PIRA by Colonel Gaddafi's Libya. In response to the devastating loss of life, the British Army declared the roads of East Tyrone off limits to its men and took to ferrying soldiers in and out of the area by helicopter.

The attack, the largest loss of military life since the Warrenpoint bombing nearly ten years previously, caused fury in Whitehall, with representatives of the British government talking darkly about the possibility of reintroducing internment for known members of the PIRA. Within days of the bombing,

Mid Ulster TCG received intelligence from a senior source in the PIRA that an ASU belonging to the East Tyrone Brigade was planning to assassinate an off-duty member of the security forces in the Carrickmore area. It cannot be known whether this intelligence was provided by the same source that prompted the Loughgall ambush or whether it was meant as a gesture to the British government to forestall the reintroduction of internment and the certain breakdown of peace negotiations that would follow. It may have been entirely coincidental that the members of the ASU involved in the planned assassination were also believed by British intelligence to have been responsible for the Ballygawley bomb. Nevertheless, it is hard not to speculate that there may have been some connection between the bombing and the offering up of this intelligence.

The target of the PIRA operation was a part-time UDR soldier who worked as a driver in his civilian life and made regular deliveries to Carrickmore RUC station and the UDR barracks in Omagh. The source intelligence gave specific details as to the identity of the intended victim but was unable to provide a firm date for the expected attack. The SAS were tasked by the TCG to deal with the situation. The Troop had learned a hard lesson from their failed ambush near Portadown in 1984 about the difficulty of coordinating mobile units in an attack on an uncooperative enemy. The use of a moving vehicle as bait for an assassination squad had, on that occasion, resulted in a running gun battle through the lanes and roads of the area, and, ultimately, to the death of an innocent civilian in the crossfire. Any kind of mobile interception of the PIRA ASU was therefore ruled out. Instead, the men of the Troop decided to lure the terrorists into a carefully planned static ambush.

On the morning of Tuesday, 30 August 1988, ten days after the Balleygawley bombing, the SAS operation swung into action. A plainclothes volunteer from the regiment took the dangerous job of bait, standing in for the intended PIRA target and driving his large blue and white lorry conspicuously around the Carrickmore area. Once he was confident that the PIRA's 'dickers' must have seen the vehicle, the driver pulled over to the side of the road from Carrickmore to Omagh and parked next to a deserted and boarded-up two-storey house. The undercover soldier then got out of the cab and set about changing a tyre, going through the motions as if one had actually blown.

Carrickmore sits in the heart of what the security forces in Ulster called 'bandit country'. The village itself was a republican stronghold with a long tradition of fierce support for the IRA. It housed a 'Garden of Remembrance' that commemorated fallen members of the movement from the Tyrone area and played host to a memorial service every Easter Sunday that drew together republicans from all across the province. It was not a comfortable place to be an exposed British soldier. The SAS man who had volunteered to act as bait for the PIRA attack knew that he was in extremely grave danger; any passing car might contain gunmen intent on ending his life in a heartbeat. There are many types of courage in the world, but this particular job took a special man and a special kind of bravery.

Inside the boarded-up shop was a four-man SAS team that had been inserted the night before. Three of the team members carried Armalites while the final man was armed with a .223 light machine-gun capable of putting down sustained bursts of heavy fire. The team had prepared the ambush site carefully in the darkness. The machine-gunner took up a firing position near the roof of the deserted building, removing some of the bricks in the wall in front of him to ensure a clear field of fire. The other men spread out through the building. Outside, another eight soldiers concealed themselves along the roadside to ensure that there would be no escape for the would-be assassins. Once everyone had settled into position, the waiting began.

The broken-down lorry was the bait, intended to draw out the PIRA hit squad. However, there was no guarantee that the ASU would be in the area that day, or that they would take the bait if they were, so all involved knew they might be consigned to a long, uncomfortable and ultimately fruitless wait. Fortunately for the ambush team, the PIRA unit was not far away and its members were intent on getting their kill.

Half a mile from the ambush site, at around two o'clock in the afternoon, three armed and masked terrorists dressed in blue boiler suits pushed their way into the family home of a local man named Justin McBride. Two of the intruders were carrying AK-47 assault rifles, while the third was armed with a .38 Webley revolver. The terrified McBride family were pushed into a back room by the PIRA men, who then closed the curtains, smashed the telephone and stole the keys to the family car, a red Fiat. The

McBride family were warned to keep quiet and not to contact the authorities before the ASU left in the stolen vehicle.

The PIRA gang drove the McBrides' Fiat a few hundred metres to the Drumnakilly road, where, at 2.05 p.m., they turned into the yard of a farmhouse belonging to the McAleer family. Two of the terrorists burst into the kitchen and ordered the elderly woman they found there into the living room. They then gathered the other occupants together, pulled down the blinds, smashed the phone and settled down to ambush their target.

A strange, long-distance standoff now ensued. The PIRA team believed that their target really had broken down and thought that they were making clever use of the time it would take to repair the vehicle. Once the truck was back on the road, they assumed, it was sure to pass through their ambush as it continued on its route. The SAS team, waiting at their own ambush site a short distance down the road, were completely unaware of this development and expected the PIRA men to come to them.

While the assassination team was waiting eagerly for the truck to start rolling again, the SAS decoy continued to pretend that he was dealing with the breakdown. Many of the motorists who passed by were kind enough to offer their assistance to the driver but the soldier nervously waved them all away. Every time a car slowed down alongside was a moment of great danger for the decoy, as it was impossible to know whether the occupants wanted to help him or to kill him. Even innocent civilians carried their own threat, since those who genuinely wished to help would increase the risk of the ambush being detected if they got out of the cars and started moving around in the killing zone.

At the McAleer house, the PIRA ASU was running into its own complications. A milkman called at 2.30 p.m. and was quickly taken prisoner by the armed men inside. Just before 3 p.m., Thaddeus McAleer drove his digger into the yard and was also swiftly apprehended. Ten minutes later, Eamon McCullough, a salesman, parked his white Sierra outside and approached the door. McCullough had come to see the McAleers about a microwave oven and had his two children in the car with him. He, his children and his car were all seized and added to the growing collection of vehicles and people being held at the farmhouse by the ASU.

The assassination team was now becoming impatient. Rather than spend more time waiting in the increasingly crowded house, they decided to abandon the ambush position and attack their target directly at the scene of the 'breakdown'. The McAleers and their unexpected guests were ordered to wait for twenty minutes before making any report to the security services. The three gunmen then commandeered Eamon McCullough's Sierra, smashing the glass out of one of the back windows to allow them to fire from the vehicle unimpeded. The two men armed with AK-47s positioned themselves in the rear of the car while the third man got into the driver's seat. Their preparations complete, the unit set off down the road intent on killing what they expected to be a helpless, unarmed and unsuspecting target.

As the white Sierra neared the ambush site, the decoy raised his eyes from the undamaged tyre in front of him and watched the vehicle approach. Initially, he was unconcerned; the Sierra appeared to be just one more civilian car among the many others that had passed by during his long wait. But as the car drew nearer, the driver suddenly swerved, turning to reveal the broken rear window in order to allow the men in the back to bring their weapons to bear. Realising that the attack was finally under way, the SAS man dropped the tyre and sprinted for the gates of the house, running literally for his life.

One of the PIRA gunmen fired a burst from his AK-47 as the soldier ran. Some of the bullets hit the lorry, while others kicked up dust around his feet, but none struck home and the decoy was able to fling himself into cover, unharmed. The SAS machine-gunner immediately opened fire on the gunman, killing him instantly. The rest of the SAS ambush team engaged the other two PIRA terrorists, riddling the stolen Sierra with bullets. Within seconds, all three members of the ASU were dead.

The driver of the vehicle was PIRA Volunteer Gerard Harte. The men in the back were Brian Mullin and Martin Harte, the brother of the driver. MI5 and RUC Special Branch both had firm intelligence that the Harte brothers had been involved in the Ballygawley bus bombing. This has always been denied by both the PIRA and the families of the dead terrorists.

Two days after the ambush, then Prime Minister Margaret Thatcher gave an interview to the *Daily Express*, addressing the killings in her usual combative style: 'When you are faced with terrorism, you obviously do not let the terrorists know precisely what steps you are taking to counter their terrorism. Nor shall we. But my message to them is this: Do not doubt our resolve to defeat terrorism.' While the citation for John McAleese's Military Medal has never been made public, well-informed sources suggest that it was awarded, in part at least, for his contribution to the ambush on the Drumnakilly road.

Since its formation in 1986, the Irish People's Liberation Army (IPLO) had been involved in a violent feud with its former comrades in the INLA, with many lives lost on both sides. In late 1989 and 1990, tensions also increased between the IPLO and the PIRA due to the IPLO's open recruitment of criminals, many of whom escaped the kangaroo court justice of the PIRA (kneecapping or punishment beatings) by joining the organisation. Despite the orgy of violence perpetrated by the IPLO, it was only proscribed by the Secretary of State for Northern Ireland on 8 March 1990. Just one month after being designated as a banned organisation, the IPLO launched an assassination attempt against an off-duty RUC officer on the outskirts of Armagh city.

In the spring of 1990, Mid Ulster TCG were informed of the impending attack by RUC Special Branch, who received their information from a paid informer inside the IPLO. The lead terrorist in the planned operation was known to be Martin Corrigan (24), married with two children. Corrigan was a former member of the PIRA who had decided to shift his allegiance to the radical left-wing group. He came from a family with deep republican roots. His father, Peter Corrigan, a member of Sinn Féin, was shot dead by a Protestant gunman in October 1982 while on his way to sign on for unemployment benefits. Ex-UDR soldier and loyalist terrorist Jeffrey Edwards was later convicted of the murder. Martin Corrigan witnessed his father's murder, finding in it good reason to take part in the violent republican campaign against both loyalists and the British state.

In the early hours of Thursday, 18 April, Corrigan, armed with an M1 Carbine and in the company of another IPLO terrorist carrying a sawn-off shotgun, approached the home of what he believed to be an unsuspecting victim. In fact, the pair were walking into a trap: an SAS ambush party, led by one of the most experienced NCOs in the regiment, was lying in wait for them. Corrigan was challenged as he approached the house and fired at the ambush party. The SAS men returned fire, killing him instantly. The second IPLO gunman surrendered and was later convicted of terrorist offences. Corrigan was the only member of the IPLO killed by security forces during the Northern Ireland Troubles.

The 1980s had been a decade of development for both the SAS and the intelligence services in Ulster. Hard lessons had been learned. As the 1980s ended and the nineties began, the SAS in Northern Ireland became sleeker, more focused and even more lethal. An important step was taken towards the end of the decade, when the regiment realised that detaching a troop to operate in Ulster from the squadron rotating through the anti-terrorist role was not the most efficient use of resources. Each time a new squadron took on the role, experienced troopers who had come to know the ground were removed wholesale and replaced with a completely new troop that had to familiarise itself afresh with the unique environment in Northern Ireland. Taking its lead from

14 Intelligence Company, a posting to Ulster became a specialist role in the SAS that anyone in the regiment could volunteer for. This meant that there was always a contingent of experienced soldiers in theatre at any given time.

The early 1990s would see an increasing focus by the intelligence services on the East Tyrone Brigade of the PIRA. It had become increasingly clear to those conducting the undercover war that the PIRA leadership were trying to steer their movement away from direct military conflict and towards a more political role. In doing so, they faced fierce opposition from some among their own ranks. The men of Tyrone, in particular, were notorious for their independent-mindedness and their willingness to challenge, and sometimes even threaten, those who were moving the PIRA in a new direction.

The Loughgall ambush had halted any immediate move by members of the East Tyrone Brigade to break away from the main provisional movement. However, despite their heavy losses, there was barely any let-up in the pace and intensity of the brigade's activities. The members of the brigade, despite having been robbed of most of their senior leadership, were still viewed as fanatical hardline militarists who would carry out operations wherever they could. The death of Seamus McElwaine had cut the heart out of the Fermanagh Brigade of the PIRA. As a consequence, attacks in County Fermanagh were increasingly carried out by the Tyrone Brigade. These attacks included the atrocity of the Enniskillen Remembrance Day bombing, which left eleven dead, including three married civilian couples.

In the coming decade, the SAS, acting on high-level source intelligence from the very top of the PIRA, would further degrade the capabilities of the East Tyrone Brigade. By the time a political compromise was reached between the republican movement and the British government, the Tyrone Brigade would be in no position to challenge its own leadership's new commitment to peace.

CHAPTER TWELVE

9 DET

THE DET (1985–95)

By the late 1980s, the operational effectiveness of the PIRA's Belfast Brigade had been diminished to such an extent that three out of every four operations launched were either aborted or compromised. These successes were due to the close cooperation of the Belfast contingent of 14 Intelligence Company with the RUC's HMSU and E4A units, working together under the auspices of the Belfast Tasking and Co-ordination Group. The combination of close surveillance and the penetration of the Belfast Brigade by dozens of informers meant that PIRA actions could often be halted before they had the chance to evolve into threats to the public or the security forces.

The vast majority of the Belfast Det's operations, mounted on the basis of sound Special Branch or FRU source intelligence, did not result in any sort of direct confrontation with PIRA members. Instead, the Det's operations led to the seizure of huge quantities of explosives and weapons, as well as the gathering of evidence for the successful arrest and prosecution of those involved in terrorist operations, logistics and planning. Often, successful surveillance and the threat of criminal charges would lead PIRA members to turn on their fellows and become informers, providing a cascade of fresh leads and further prosecutions. One former Special Branch officer estimates that, between 1985 and 1995, about one in every twenty members of the Belfast PIRA was an informer for either the RUC or military intelligence.

The ongoing degradation of the Belfast Brigade's operational effectiveness, and the frequency with which its members were being turned, caused a serious morale problem within the organisation. An almost hysterical paranoia set in within the various regional subunits throughout the city, with tensions rising as leaders and rank-and-file members began to see informers everywhere. During this period, the PIRA's own internal security unit executed suspected informers on an unprecedented scale. Over seventy PIRA members would be executed on dubious grounds by their own comrades during the Troubles, with the rate of killings at times outstripping the casualties inflicted by the security forces.

Despite these successes, the members of the Belfast Det knew that the situation in the city was far from stable and that the PIRA maintained the ability to inflict serious casualties on the security forces. While assistance from the RUC's E4A unit was regularly available, there were simply never enough operators in the Belfast Det to both carry out routine surveillance and respond to major operations when called for. It was clear that more eyes were required on the ground and this manpower need led directly to the formation of a completely new Det – 9 Det – in the late 1980s and early 1990s.

Specifically, 9 Det was raised to assist the Belfast Det in its covert fight against the PIRA. In order to meet the urgent requirements of the situation, recruiting rules were modified for the new unit. Previously, serving members of other Special Forces units were not permitted to apply for 14 Intelligence Company training, to avoid the problem of the 'cannibalisation' of units whose members were already in extremely high demand. Now, for the first time, members of the SAS and the SBS were allowed to volunteer for a two-year tour with the new Det unit as surveillance operators. Many did.

As in Belfast, PIRA activity in Northern Ireland's second city, Londonderry, had been effectively degraded through a combination of coordinated source intelligence, surveillance and police arrests. This left two major hotbeds of PIRA activity in the province: Tyrone and South Armagh. Between 1985 and 1995, South Armagh was an intelligence desert for the security services. With no well-placed informers in the region, there was little information on which surveillance operations could build, so the security services were largely relegated to a defensive and reactive role. Ironically, this situation only began to change when the PIRA announced a ceasefire in 1994, which finally created the conditions for the penetration of this most formidable of the PIRA's regional brigades.

The situation in East Tyrone was different. Mid Ulster TCG continued to receive accurate high-level intelligence on the East

Tyrone Brigade and the Mid Ulster Det was at the forefront of the increasing effort to leverage this information in order to further degrade the brigade's capacity for violent action. However, despite the successes at Loughgall in 1987 and at Drumnakilly the following year, operating in Tyrone remained extremely dangerous. This was graphically illustrated on 24 March 1990, when two operators from the Mid Ulster Det narrowly escaped from an ambush near the republican stronghold of Cappagh, County Tyrone.

Mid Ulster TCG had received reliable intelligence that a PIRA ASU was preparing for an attack in the area. While the intelligence came from a reliable source, it provided no specific facts about the planned attack. Det operators were sent into the area to carry out surveillance on the most likely suspects in order to fill in the blanks. Unfortunately, one of the Det cars was 'blown' during the course of the operation. Once they had identified the vehicle as belonging to the security forces, local PIRA members attempted to ambush the car. The ambush was unsuccessful. The two Det operators in the vehicle returned fire with their car weapons and fought their way out of the potentially deadly trap. Neither operator was injured in the engagement but one of the PIRA men was shot and wounded during the firefight.

The PIRA announced that they had killed two SAS soldiers in the ambush. While this claim had no foundation in reality, it did provide fuel for some rather overactive imaginations. Even today, some more conspiratorially-minded republicans believe that a car crash in Germany later in the week was used to cover up the deaths from a successful PIRA operation. The truth is that there was no point during the Troubles at which the British government withheld the truth about the many military lives that were lost in Ulster. Given that there were only two operators in the Det car, if the ambush had killed both men, the PIRA should have had no difficulties in producing evidence of the deaths.

The spreading by the PIRA of misinformation about engagements had become habitual by this point, as they saw considerable value in casting into doubt whatever the British government had to say about any matter at all. However, in this particular case the misinformation may have been intended to deflect attention from the PIRA's own casualties. It must have been a matter of some embarrassment to them that, even when they controlled the timing, location and numbers involved in an engagement, they were utterly outmatched if the opponent was able to fight back.

The wounded PIRA man, Martin McCaughey, served as a member of the Borough Council in South Tyrone, where he had been elected as a Sinn Féin candidate. McCaughey was dismissed from his role on the council after failing to attend a required monthly meeting. It was later discovered that the reason for his absence was that he had been spirited across the border into the Republic to receive treatment for the wounds he sustained in the Cappagh ambush. McCaughey's narrow escape did nothing to deter him from the path of violence. Two months later, he would meet actual SAS soldiers outside a mushroom shed near Loughgall. The outcome of this second engagement would not be so fortunate for him.

In the middle of the afternoon on 2 September 1989, a rare bright autumn day, a motorcycle carrying two men approached the Ardoyne shop fronts in north Belfast. The shop fronts were a flash point for clashes between residents of the Protestant Woodvale and Catholic Ardoyne areas of the city. On the rear of the motorcycle was a local man named Brian Robinson. Robinson was a member of the outlawed Ulster Volunteer Force (UVF). Like the PIRA, the UVF aped the kind of formal military structures used by the British Army and, according to their organisational system, Robinson belonged to B Company of the 1st Battalion of the UVF's Belfast Brigade. Despite all the militaristic trappings, Robinson was nothing more than a terrorist thug. Armed with an automatic weapon, he set out that afternoon with just one intention: to kill a member of the Catholic community. He had no intention of finding a target with links to the PIRA – any Catholic would do.

As the motorcycle came close to the local chemists, it began to slow down. A small group of people were approaching the shop up ahead. Paddy McKenna, a Catholic with no connection to any terrorist organisation, was walking along the pavement with a female friend, leading a two-year-old girl behind them. The motorcycle pulled to a halt a few paces behind them and Robinson jumped off the back. Knocking the little girl aside in his haste to reach his target, Robinson raised his weapon and shot McKenna eleven times, killing him instantly. As McKenna slumped to the concrete floor, his killer climbed back onto the rear of the motorcycle. The bike, driven by fellow UVF member

Davy McCullough, sped off down the Crumlin Road intending to escape quickly into the streets of the Woodvale area.

Unfortunately for the UVF assassination team, two members of the newly formed 9 Det, one a female operator and the other a volunteer from the Special Boat Service, were on routine surveillance duties in the area in an unmarked Vauxhall Astra and witnessed the shooting. They immediately gave chase. The SBS operator put his foot to the floor and took off after the motorcycle at breakneck speed, quickly closing the distance to the fleeing killers. As the car approached, Robinson became aware that he was being pursued. The UVF man turned on the pillion seat and brought his weapon to bear on the Astra.

Fearing that they were about to come under fire, the Det operator sped up and rammed the motorcycle. Robinson, still armed, was knocked onto the bonnet of the Det car, sliding off as the vehicle lurched to a halt. The impact of the crash momentarily stunned the two operators in the car. Meanwhile, Robinson pulled himself up and staggered away towards a nearby bus shelter.

The female operator recovered her composure first and leaped out of the passenger-side door. Believing that Robinson was still armed, she drew her 9mm Browning and engaged the gunman, hitting him several times and knocking him to the floor. A moment later, the second operator emerged from the driver's side of the car. Despite his wounds, Robinson continued to move about on the ground. Seeing a jerking movement of his hand near the waist area, the operator took the instant decision that the terrorist might still represent a threat and could be reaching for a weapon in his waistband. The operator fired at least three more shots into the head of the downed terrorist, killing him.

The second UVF terrorist, Davy McCullough, was badly injured in the collision between the two vehicles. He was arrested by RUC officers at the scene and taken to hospital. Robinson's mother was informed of her son's death later in the day. On hearing the news, she dropped to the ground, the victim of a fatal heart attack. Paddy McKenna, an innocent man who was killed for no other reason than that he was a Catholic, was buried on the same day as his killer.

The response to the killings in the loyalist and republican communities offers a clear example of the impossible situation the British military often faced in Northern Ireland. Despite committing a senseless sectarian murder, Robinson was treated as a hero by the loyalists. Hundreds turned out for his funeral and his death is still commemorated today with a mural in his honour on Belfast's Disraeli Street. There was fury in loyalist circles that one of their men had been killed by British forces while he was, in their view, 'fighting' to protect the union. Relatively few loyalist terrorists were killed by the security forces during the Troubles because, in almost all cases, they surrendered peacefully rather than raising weapons against British soldiers or policemen. Robinson's killing was a rare occasion on which a loyalist had turned a gun on the security forces and the consequences for him were exactly the same as those faced by republicans terrorists who pursued the same course. Nevertheless, at least some loyalists continue to believe that Robinson was wronged: in 2015, his son

Robert tore down an SAS flag, raised by other loyalists in north Belfast, in an act of protest at the killing of his father.

Meanwhile, on the other side of the divide, the republican community maintains that Paddy McKenna and Brian Robinson were both sacrificed by the UVF as part of a propaganda effort to make the British military look good. The UVF source for this claim alleged that British military intelligence operatives had been informed of the impending attack and that Robinson was under surveillance when he carried out his murder. The British forces present supposedly allowed the killing to be carried out (for some unexplained reason) and then killed Robinson to 'balance out' the IRA men who had been killed in recent years.

There is no truth whatsoever to this absurd claim and nor does the claimed sequence of events stand up to the simplest logical scrutiny. Not only were the security services perfectly capable of disrupting loyalist terrorist activities without being 'gifted' information if they should have wished to engineer a killing, but the idea that allowing an innocent Catholic to die would provide better propaganda than saving him does not bear a moment's consideration. Perhaps most importantly, the entire fiction is predicated on the idea that the soldiers involved belonged to the SAS or a similar organisation. Anyone familiar with the Det knows that it acted as a dedicated surveillance organisation that did everything in its power to avoid being involved in contacts, since these were fundamentally at odds with its mission. The truth is simply that a pair of Det operators were carrying out routine surveillance on a known flashpoint, witnessed a killing that happened too quickly for them to prevent and then engaged the murderers as they fled. Sadly, neither republicans nor loyalists are known for letting reality get in the way of a good conspiracy theory concerning the British state.

There has also been some public criticism of the operators involved for either 'shooting to kill' or engaging in unnecessary 'overkill' during the shooting of Brian Robinson. The primary source of this criticism has been the decision made by the second operator to shoot Robinson in the head while he was already lying on the ground. It is always easy, in the cold light of day and with mature reflection, to make such accusations. Those who do so ignore the fact that both Det operators had, just moments before, witnessed Robinson commit a cold-blooded murder, gunning down an innocent on the street. Both also believed that he might still be armed and was, thus, a danger to each of them. In the heat of a combat situation even the slightest movement can be misinterpreted, especially if you think your life may be in danger. Indeed, it is questionable whether we should even talk of misinterpretation. The correct response to any movement that might possibly lead to a threat is to shoot, unless you can be absolutely certain that the individual is unarmed or means no harm. Those who illegally arm themselves and set out to murder lose the right to any benefit of the doubt. There is no question that soldiers or policemen should take the risk upon themselves in order to provide a greater chance of life to such individuals.

Another Det operation from this period that still continues to cause controversy today took place in Lurgan, County Armagh, in March of 1990. Source intelligence received by the

Mid Ulster TCG in the late 1980s had identified Colin Duffy as a leading figure in the Armagh PIRA. However, Duffy proved to be an extremely difficult target to monitor, as he regularly moved locations and carried out other anti-surveillance measures to protect himself.

In January 1990, Duffy found himself caught up in an RUC raid on the home of republican activist Tony McCaughey, whom he was visiting at the time. Also present was Sam Marshall, a long-time Sinn Féin activist who had been imprisoned in his youth for his role in an arson attack. On entering McCaughey's home, the RUC officers discovered a small quantity of ammunition and arrested the three men present. All three were set free on bail shortly afterwards but as part of their bail conditions were required to sign a register at Lurgan RUC station on a regular basis.

Seeing this as an excellent opportunity to pick up Duffy's trail and to monitor him more closely, the Mid Ulster Det was tasked to carry out a major surveillance operation against the three men. When the men were due to sign the register, two plainclothes Det operators took over the observation post at the entrance of the police station and, using sophisticated camera equipment, took clear, close-up photos of the PIRA suspects as they arrived at and left the building. Meanwhile, four other Det operators in cars circled the roads around the RUC station, ready to follow the targets if they departed in vehicles. Two further operators, in plainclothes and on foot, were assigned to follow the targets as they walked away from the station.

At around 7.30 p.m. on the evening of Wednesday, 7 March, Duffy, Marshall, and McCaughey arrived at the RUC station to sign their bail. Up-to-date photographs were taken by the men in the observation post, then, as planned, the two Det operators on foot outside picked up the suspects as they left the station and followed them down the street. The three men were about 100 metres from the station when all hell broke loose. A car carrying a UVF assassination team sped towards the men and suddenly screeched to a halt nearby. Two gunmen, one armed with a South African-made AK-47, jumped out and let loose a burst of automatic fire from close range. The poorly aimed shots missed Duffy and McCaughey, but Sam Marshall was struck and fatally injured.

The two Det operators following on foot witnessed the attack but were too far away to engage the UVF terrorists. The two gunmen quickly jumped back into their car and accelerated away from the scene. The Det operators radioed in the attack on their personal radios, directing the nearest surveillance car towards the RUC station in a bid to intercept the fleeing loyalist terrorists. Unfortunately, as the Det car drove towards the scene of the shooting down one road, the UVF gunmen escaped towards Belfast along a parallel street. The other Det cars closing in on the unexpected incident were unable to pick up the trail and the UVF killers escaped. The weapons used in the attack were never recovered but ballistics evidence linked them to at least three other UVF killings.

The shooting of Sam Marshall by the UVF has fuelled countless allegations that it was the result of a conspiracy between

British undercover units and loyalist terrorists, with the surveillance teams colluding with the UVF to allow the attack to happen. The reality is that the Det operators, armed only with their 9mm pistols, were simply too far away to effectively engage the gunmen. That they would have done so if they were in range is clearly illustrated by 9 Det's shooting of the UVF killer Brian Robinson. Of course, if the operators on the ground that evening had shot or captured the loyalist gunmen, there is little doubt that the PIRA would once again have claimed that this too was the result of collusion and that the UVF men had been 'sacrificed' to improve the Army's reputation.

Colin Duffy continued to live a charmed life after the attempt to kill him. In the years prior to the Good Friday Agreement, he was arrested and charged with murder on two occasions, for the killing of a former UDR man in 1995 and the murder of two on-duty RUC officers in 1997. He was acquitted in the first case while charges were dropped in the second. After the ending of the PIRA's military campaign, Duffy was suspected of involvement in a number of terrorist actions carried out by dissident republican terrorists. In March 2009, Duffy was charged with the murder of two British soldiers outside Massereene Barracks in Antrim, the first deaths of British servicemen in the province since the PIRA had laid down their arms over a decade earlier. Despite DNA evidence linking him to a car used in the attack, Duffy was acquitted in 2012 of the charges against him after arguing that the evidence could have been planted. Later that year, Duffy was questioned in relation to the killing of prison officer David Black but was not charged. In the aftermath of Black's murder, the security services stepped up their surveillance of Duffy.

In December 2013, Duffy was arrested again and charged with involvement in a dissident gun attack on a police convoy in north Belfast and with preparing and directing terrorist operations. Duffy was brought to trial in 2019, with the prosecution alleging that video and audio surveillance show him and two other men in a public park discussing terrorist operations. The material, amounting to over 40 hours of recordings, was gathered from some 14 audio surveillance devices and video cameras located around the park. Duffy and his co-defendants deny all the charges against them. At the time of writing, the case is ongoing; Colin Duffy has never been convicted of any terrorist offence.

On 13 January 1990, two members of the SAS on secondment to 9 Det were conducting a routine surveillance patrol in west Belfast when they observed a red car pulling up outside Sean Graham's bookmakers on the Falls Road. Two hooded men burst from the car, one armed with a Second World War-era Schmeisser submachine gun and the other with a pistol. The pair ran together into the betting shop, leaving the driver of the car behind in the vehicle, ready to make their getaway when they returned. The two Det operators assumed they had stumbled upon either a UVF or a PIRA hit team going into action. The only words exchanged between the pair as they moved to intercept were spoken by the driver. He turned to his companion and said, simply, 'Here we go.'

The operators quickly pulled up beside the parked vehicle and leaped out, carrying their weapons with them. One, armed with a 9mm Browning pistol, rushed to the front driver-side door of the suspected terrorist car while his partner covered him with a Heckler & Koch MP5. As the first operator approached the vehicle, the driver inside made a sudden movement. Believing that the man was reaching for a gun, the operator fired a quick sequence of shots, hitting his target six times and killing him almost instantly. Seconds later, the two hooded gunmen who had been inside the shop ran out onto the street, brandishing their weapons. Both operators immediately engaged the gunmen. The soldier armed with the MP5 fired first, knocking both targets to the floor. Seeing that the men still had hold of their weapons, and assuming that they still remained a danger, the second operator fired deliberate shots at each man with his Browning, killing them both.

Conscious that they were on the street with no backup in an extremely hostile area, the operators recovered the weapons from the bodies of the gunmen and jumped back into their car to remove themselves from the scene of the contact as quickly as possible. As they tried to drive away, a pair of black taxis ahead of them on the road moved to block their escape, forcing the Det driver to mount the pavement in order to bypass the improvised roadblock. The gap between the Det car and the nearest black taxi was so narrow that the wing mirrors of both vehicles were smashed off as the Det car swept by. Despite the cosmetic damage, the two operators now had open road ahead of them and accelerated rapidly away, driving out of Catholic west Belfast and onto the Shankill Road.

As the two Det operators hurried along the Shankill, believing that the drama of the day was over, they saw that the road ahead was sealed off by an RUC checkpoint. Bringing their unmarked car to a halt, the driver wound down his window and prepared to explain to the approaching policeman what had just happened at the bookmakers. Before he had a chance to identify himself, the policeman's personal radio crackled into life and the driver overheard a transmission reporting the shooting on the Falls Road. As he listened to the description of the car suspected of involvement in a triple murder, the operator realised that it was his own vehicle being described. The RUC Constable came to the same conclusion at the same moment and instantly dropped his hand to the police issue .357 Ruger revolver at his belt. One of the operators later informed the author that this was the first time he had truly felt scared that day. The operators froze, keeping their hands visible, and shouted out that they were British soldiers. Fortunately, the RUC men manning the roadblock had cool heads and proceeded to formally identify the pair as members of the security forces. A potential 'blue on blue' tragedy had been averted.

The Det men were escorted to the nearby Tennant Street RUC station to give an account of the earlier events. A police weapons expert was also called in to examine the two firearms that had been seized after the shooting. He took one look at the weapons, glanced up at the operators and shrugged apologetically: 'Sorry, lads. No serial numbers.' The weapons the gunmen had been carrying were harmless replicas.

The men shot by the 9 Det operators were Peter Thompson (21), Edward Paul Hale (25) and John Joseph McNeill (42). None of the men was a member of any loyalist or republican terrorist organisation, but all were known to the police for their involvement in a long string of criminal offences, including burglary. The only one of the three who could be connected to the PIRA in any way was Edward Hale, but that was as the victim of a 'punishment shooting' carried out in retaliation for 'anti-social behaviour' rather than because he was affiliated in any way to the republican cause. The three men, it turned out, had been engaged in an armed robbery when they were interdicted by the 9 Det team. Sources close to their gang later suggested that the driver was supposed to bang on the metal grille covering the front of the betting shop to warn his accomplices inside if a police or army patrol approached. It is believed that when the Det operators shot the driver of the car outside, the reverberations from the gunshots caused the grille to shake. The robbers inside, thinking this was their warning signal, ran back through the door and straight into the sights of the undercover soldiers outside.

The shooting by armed soldiers of three men with no terrorist affiliations led to intense media scrutiny of the events that took place that day. The legality of the use of lethal force was widely questioned, particularly with respect to the shooting of the driver, since no gun of any kind was found inside the car. Given that some still insist, despite the decision of two coroner's inquiries held in front of juries, that the killings were unlawful, it is perhaps helpful to step back for a moment and consider the law surrounding acts of self-defence, which underpinned all uses of lethal force by undercover soldiers and police officers during the conflict in Ulster.

Self-defence is defined by Section 3 of the Criminal Law Act 1967 as follows:

> A person may use such force as is reasonable in the circum-
> stances in the prevention of crime, or in effecting or assisting
> in the lawful arrest of offenders or suspected offenders or of
> persons unlawfully at large.

This definition is deliberately vague because it is meant to encom-pass all possible instances of self-defence and what may be reason-able in one set of circumstances may not be reasonable in another. Both the House of Lords and the present Supreme Court have declined to clarify the law any further than the 1967 Act. When any court of law considers the circumstances in which lethal force has been used, it must consider the facts as they appeared to the person who used lethal force and thus assess what he or she honestly believed those facts to be. The 'honest belief' in such cases does not have to be reasonable, only honestly held.

Applying the law of self-defence to the shooting of Hale, Thompson and McNeill, the following is clear. Both 9 Det operators had an honest belief that they were dealing with a terrorist incident involving either a PIRA or a UVF assassina-tion team. Both honestly believed that the terrorists they were about to confront were armed and that at least one of them was carrying a functioning automatic weapon. When the 9 Det operator approached John Joseph McNeill in the car outside the bookmakers, he honestly believed both that McNeill was a terrorist and that he was armed. In those few adrenaline-fuelled seconds, any movement by McNeill, who was undoubtedly startled by the sudden approach of the Det operator, could be honestly (and reasonably) misconstrued by the Det operator as a movement towards a weapon. The use of lethal force in such a situation is lawful.

The shooting of Hale and Thompson by the second Det operator, who was suddenly confronted by two hooded and armed men who he believed to be terrorists, would unquestionably be justified as lawful self-defence. Criticism has focused instead on the actions of the first operator for continuing to shoot the pair of robbers once they were already on the ground. How, some have asked, could this possibly be justified as self-defence? Exactly the same concerns were raised at the inquest into the Gibraltar shootings and it is instructive to consider the explanation given there by an SAS officer:

It is only by shooting in the head and only by piercing the brain that one can put a stop to all movement.

Both the SAS and 14 Intelligence Company specifically train to continue shooting until there is no movement. One reason for this is that terrorists frequently use body armour of one kind or another. The other is that experience has taught both units the hard way that a wounded terrorist is just as dangerous as one who is unharmed, if not more so.

Applying the law of self-defence to the first operator's use of lethal force, we can say that he honestly believed the men were terrorists and that he honestly believed they were still a threat because they were still armed. In addition, the two Det operators were in an extremely hostile area. Had they paused to give the matter considered and studied reflection, they may well have placed themselves in considerable further danger. Given these honest beliefs, and the danger involved in waiting before taking action, the continued use of lethal force can be justified even though the targeted men were already on the ground. For these reasons, Northern Ireland's Director of Public Prosecutions (DPP) correctly declined to prosecute either of the two 9 Det operators for their actions outside Sean Graham's bookmakers on 13 January 1990.

CHAPTER THIRTEEN

THE REAPING
MACHINE

THE SAS (1990–97)

By 1989, the East Tyrone Brigade of the PIRA had become deeply concerned, almost paranoid in fact, about informers betraying their operations to the security forces. The devastating losses at Loughgall in 1987 and on the Drumnakilly road in 1988 had been inflicted by deployed and waiting SAS units. It was clear to the East Tyrone men that the security forces had sources with access to their most sensitive operational information. However, despite their best efforts, the leaders of the brigade had been unable to flush out the mole.

In an attempt to bypass the threat of treachery, an independent flying column was created in 1989 of the type that had been envisioned by Jim Lynagh. To insulate the column from the possibility that there might be an informer among the leadership of the brigade, command was given to Thomas 'Slab' Murphy, former commander of the South Armagh Brigade and reputedly a sometime member of the PIRA's ruling Army Council. The aim of the flying column was to launch a large-scale military attack on a British Army installation.

On 13 December 1989, Murphy's men carried out what may have been the most sophisticated republican military operation since the War of Independence. The target was the British Army base at the Derryard checkpoint in Fermanagh, used to watch over and control the traffic that flowed across the border with the Republic. The small base housed eight men from the King's Own Scottish Borderers (KOSB), along with an RUC officer to provide civil policing oversight for traffic stops. The base consisted of a number of small defensive positions along with a building to provide living quarters for the men.

Murphy's attacking force included some twenty PIRA volunteers, organised in military fashion into an assault group and cut-off groups. The men assigned to the cut-off groups secured the roads leading towards the checkpoint in order to prevent reinforcements arriving, keep civilians out of the combat zone and ensure that the soldiers in the base could not easily retreat. Once the cut-offs were in place, the assault team approached the checkpoint in a converted Bedford truck. The vehicle had been specially prepared for the operation, fitted with rudimentary armour under its canvas sides to provide protection from incoming fire. The eleven PIRA men inside the truck were armed to the teeth with the finest weaponry that Colonel Gaddafi's Libya could offer.

In addition to a full complement of assault rifles, grenades and RPG-7s, a pair of DshK heavy machine-guns were also mounted on firing points fixed to the flatbed of the truck. In addition, in what was probably the only use of such a weapon in anger at any time in the UK, a Soviet LPO-50 flamethrower was mounted on the vehicle, ready to spit burning fuel into the British defensive positions. Following some distance behind the truck was a van carrying a 400lb bomb, the *coup de grâce* that would destroy the installation once the defenders had been neutralised.

The heavily-armed PIRA assault team put in their attack at dusk, approaching the British base just after 4 p.m., as the winter darkness began to draw in. The truck rolled to a halt at the checkpoint, initially appearing to be nothing more than another vehicle seeking to cross the border. One of the soldiers on duty moved to the rear of the truck to check its contents, triggering the first shots of the engagement. Private James Houston was killed immediately by a fusillade of fire from inside the vehicle. The PIRA men then turned their attention to the base defences.

The storm of fire unleashed by the PIRA column was ferocious. Explosions echoed as grenades were thrown into the perimeter, RPGs smashed into the observation tower and the flamethrower lit up the evening gloom as the men inside the truck directed its stream of fire at one of the defensive positions. With the British soldiers caught off guard and rushing for shelter, the Bedford smashed its way through the gates into the interior of the base. All the while, the men inside the vehicle continued to pour a heavy fire into the buildings where the Borderers were sheltering.

The men of the garrison fired back at their attackers but were effectively pinned down, unable to manoeuvre to prepare a counterattack. Fortunately for them, a four-man KOSB fire-team patrolling the countryside near the base rushed towards the sound of the guns and quickly put themselves in a position to threaten the PIRA assault team's rear. Concerned about the possibility of having their retreat cut off, the PIRA field commander made the decision to withdraw. The truck pulled out of the compound and was replaced by the van carrying its 400lb bomb. Having set a timer on the explosives, the flying column fell back across the border into the Republic, leaving a scene of devastation behind them. Fortunately for those remaining in the compound, the main explosive charge in the van failed to detonate.

Incredibly, other than Private Houston, who had fallen in the first moments of the engagement, only one other soldier was killed: Lance Corporal Michael Paterson. Two soldiers were also wounded. Corporal Robert Duncan, the NCO commanding the garrison, was awarded the Distinguished Conduct Medal for his part in the action, while Corporal Ian Harvey also received a DCM for leading the relief force that ultimately drove off the attackers.

While the flying column was under the overall command of Slab Murphy, the attack itself was led by Tyrone man Pete Ryan, a PIRA member notorious for taking part in an armed breakout from the Crumlin Road Gaol in 1981. Unconfirmed intelligence reports at the time suggested that the assault team may also have received training prior to the attack by a former member of the Parachute Regiment who had defected to the PIRA. Whether or not this was the case, the operation bore the hallmarks of aggressive daring that would have made any Para commander proud.

Neither Army nor RUC intelligence services had received the slightest warning of the attack on the Derryard checkpoint and senior officers were stunned by the professionalism and ferocity of the attack. Pete Ryan and Slab Murphy had shown that, with sufficient internal security measures in place, a PIRA unit could successfully implement James Lynagh's vision and carry the war to the British. It now became a matter of urgency to the security services to locate and neutralise Ryan before he could take up Lynagh's mantel and shift the parameters of the conflict in the province.

In October 1990, Mid Ulster TCG received intelligence from a high-level source within the PIRA that two AK-47 rifles were being stored in a mushroom shed near Loughgall. The source reported that the weapons were to be collected from the arms dump by two of the most wanted terrorists in Tyrone, who intended to use them to attack a security force target nearby to avenge the SAS ambush that had taken place in the town three years earlier. One of the men, Martin McCaughey, had only recently recovered from the gunshot wounds he had sustained in the attempted ambush of 14 Intelligence Company operators near Cappagh, two months earlier. The other man, Desmond 'Dessie' Grew, had his own very personal reasons for wanting to give the British a bloody nose.

Grew had been born into an extremely active republican family and had witnessed the devastating effects of sectarian violence at first hand. His family had been burned out of their home in a Protestant neighbourhood, forcing them to move to a village in County Armagh. Here, the family home was again destroyed by local Protestants in a bomb attack that wounded six of the family's eleven children. Perhaps unsurprisingly, Dessie, along with his brothers Seamus and Aiden, was drawn into the orbit of 'physical force' republicanism, joining first the old Official IRA and then its splinter faction, the INLA.

In 1982, Seamus Grew was one of those killed in the spate of controversial shootings by members of the RUC's HMSU that led to the setting up of the Stalker inquiry. His brother Aiden joined the PIRA. Aiden was captured by the RUC in 1984 following a shoot-out as he attempted to escape from the scene of a bomb attack on a UDR vehicle. He received a fifteen-year sentence for his role in the bombing. The security services believe that Aiden Grew became a senior member of the dissident Real IRA in the aftermath of the Good Friday Agreement. He was convicted of cigarette smuggling in 2005.

Dessie Grew remained an active member of the INLA through-out the 1980s, during which time he was suspected of involvement in a number of murders. Eventually, in response to the internal feuds within the organisation, he switched his allegiance to the PIRA. Grew was a hardline republican and a committed opponent of the Adams/McGuinness faction's goal of achieving a political settlement with the British government.

Mid Ulster TCG tasked 14 Intelligence Company to carry out a detailed surveillance of the mushroom shed in which the PIRA arms dump was concealed. Det operators quickly established that the two AK-47s and a quantity of ammunition were present and an SAS ambush party was inserted to watch the location. On the night of 9 October 1990, Grew and McCaughey entered the shed and armed themselves. As they left the building, the SAS team moved to intercept them. In the ensuing contact, the SAS men blanketed their targets with a heavy fire. McCaughey had been fortunate to escape alive from his earlier clash with the Det. Now his luck ran out. When examined later, his body was found to have been hit by twelve rounds fired by the ambush team. Grew was shot forty-eight times. An inquest concluded that the SAS team had used reasonable force in engaging the two armed terrorists. In 2017, judges on the Court of Appeal rejected an attempt to have the inquest verdict quashed.

In November 1990, an RUC Special Branch source informed his handler that the INLA were planning to kill an off-duty UDR soldier in the village of Victoria Bridge, near Strabane in County Tyrone. The SAS were tasked to deal with the assassination attempt. The soldier and his family were moved to a safe location and an SAS team inserted into place.

On 12 November, three INLA terrorists drove past the UDR man's home in the village of Victoria Bridge, intending to rake it with automatic gunfire. One of the men opened fire from the rear of the vehicle with an automatic weapon, firing six shots into the house. As the terrorists tried to make their escape, the SAS ambush team opened fire. The driver of the car was shot dead as he attempted to regain control of the vehicle after mistiming a bend. The other two INLA terrorists fled on foot but were captured nearby.

The dead man was later identified as INLA terrorist Alex Patterson. Patterson was, ironically, an RUC Special Branch informer, indeed the very man who had provided the intelligence that led to the ambush. His death caused a great deal of friction between Special Branch and the SAS. Special Branch, unsurprisingly, were unhappy at the loss of a valued source. The SAS men involved in the operation, on the other hand, thought it ridiculous that anyone should expect them to be able to pick out and avoid individuals in a firefight involving a moving vehicle and automatic weapons.

The Mid Ulster ambushes of October and November 1990 were notable successes, chipping away at the capabilities of the terrorist organisations operating in the area. Another major blow was struck in June of the following year, this time leaving three members of the East Tyrone Brigade dead. Not only did this operation destroy a PIRA ASU but it also helped to quell a particularly vicious cycle of sectarian killings.

The SAS operation was the capstone on a sequence of violence that stretched back to April 1988, when a young UDR soldier from Coagh named Edward Gibson was murdered while working his regular job in nearby Ardboe. The village of Coagh was unusual for having a largely Protestant population, while the surrounding area of County Tyrone was predominantly Catholic. The local Protestant community viewed Gibson's killing as a direct attack on them by the PIRA. Later that year, a UVF unit carried out a revenge attack, murdering Catholic civilian Phelim McNally in Ardboe. The likely target of the attack was Phelim's brother,

Francis McNally, a local Sinn Féin councillor. Six months later, in March 1989, the PIRA responded with a drive-by shooting on a business in Coagh owned by a former UDR soldier. The owner, Leslie Dallas, was killed in the attack, as were two pensioners who were visiting at the time: Austin Nelson (62) and Ernie Rankin (72).

The indiscriminate nature of the shootings at Dallas's garage shifted the spiral of violence into a higher gear. The UVF responded later in the year with their own atrocity, bursting into the crowded Battery Bar in Ardboe and shooting dead Liam Ryan, a senior member of the PIRA, as well as a civilian named Michael Devlin. Another civilian was shot five times during the attack but survived his injuries. The PIRA responded in March 1990 with the killing of another UDR man, Thomas Jamison. Almost exactly a year later, on 3 March 1991, the UVF struck back with an attack on a pub deep in republican territory. Three members of a PIRA ASU – Dwayne O'Connell (17), Malcolm Nugent (20) and John Quinn (23) – were killed in their vehicle as they pulled into the car park of Boyle's Bar in the village of Cappagh. The UVF terrorists then fired at random into the building itself, killing one civilian, Thomas Armstrong, and badly wounding another.

The killing of a complete ASU in a village considered to be a republican stronghold was not an event the East Tyrone Brigade were prepared to take lightly. Intent on a quick response, one month later, a PIRA unit shot dead Protestant builder Derek Ferguson while he sat at home in Coagh watching television with his children. Ferguson was the cousin of Mid Ulster Member of

Parliament and unionist politician Reverend William McCrea. However, the killing of a single Protestant, even one with family ties to the loyalist establishment, was not enough to balance the books. More blood would have to be spilled, so the PIRA began to lay plans for a second attack.

Mid Ulster TCG received intelligence from a high-level source that the East Tyrone Brigade intended to carry out an attack on another off-duty UDR soldier in Coagh. According to the source, the attack would be led by Pete Ryan, the man who had commanded the spectacular assault on the Derryard checkpoint. Operators from 14 Intelligence Company immediately began an intensive surveillance operation and quickly established that Ryan's assassination team would include Lawrence McNally and Tony Doris.

Lawrence McNally was a veteran of the 'bandit country' conflict and one of the East Tyrone Brigade's top gunmen. McNally's history with the unit stretched back over a decade. In 1980, he had been tried and acquitted in Dublin for the murder of a former UDR soldier, Henry Livingstone, and he had remained on the radar of the security services ever since. McNally had personal reasons for wanting to be involved in Ryan's planned revenge attack: Phelim McNally, the first Catholic civilian to be killed in the cycle of violence, had been his brother.

At twenty-one years of age, Tony Doris was much younger than his fellow volunteers, but had risen fast through the ranks since joining the PIRA at seventeen. In just four years he had impressed the brigade leadership enough to be appointed as commander of the Coalisland Company. Doris was an active and dedicated republican who had been arrested numerous times on suspicion of involvement in terrorist activity. He is believed to have been involved in a number of shootings and some republican sources suggest that he was part of the unit responsible for the drive-by attack on Leslie Dallas's garage in Coagh. There is no doubt that Ryan had assembled a hardened and experienced team of killers for the job he was planning.

As the intelligence about Ryan's plans firmed up, the SAS were deployed to Coagh. The commander of the operation once again opted to use a decoy, with a member of the team who bore a passing resemblance to the target taking the place of the intended victim. On 2 June, the evening before the attack, the PIRA ASU hijacked a red Vauxhall Cavalier in the nearby village of Moneymore. Unbeknown to the terrorists, the hijacking was observed by 14 Intelligence Company operators assigned to follow the men. Close surveillance teams mounted a constant watch over Ryan and his gang throughout the night and at 7.30 a.m. the following morning radioed in the information that the ASU was on the move and headed out of Moneymore. Det cars followed as Tony Doris drove the stolen Cavalier through the countryside on the short journey towards Coagh.

The SAS ambush party was concealed inside a lorry, parked where Coagh's narrow Main Street enters the village over a bridge across the Ballinderry River. The decoy, meanwhile, waited in his car nearby, pretending to be following the UDR target's normal routine. The PIRA assassination team drove across the bridge and approached what they thought was their unwitting victim, passing within metres of the concealed SAS men. The soldiers waited until Ryan and McNally wound down the windows on their hijacked car and lifted their weapons. As soon as the threat of immediate danger to the decoy's life was clear, the SAS team opened fire from their concealed position, pouring a barrage of rounds into the approaching vehicle.

As the hail of gunfire struck the Cavalier, the vehicle careened out of control. The car, struck by some 200 bullets, smashed into a VW Golf parked nearby and immediately burst into flames. All three of the terrorists inside were killed in the brief contact. One of the rifles recovered from the burned-out vehicle was found to have been used in the 1989 killings of Leslie Dallas, Austin Nelson and Ernie Rankin just 200 yards from the scene of the SAS ambush.

The PIRA's propaganda arm later claimed that two of the men escaped the vehicle but were then executed in the street in cold blood and dragged back to the car, which was set on fire to conceal the evidence. Unsurprisingly, no eyewitnesses have ever come forward to support these claims. One need only consider the narrowness of the road, the fact that the SAS team were firing automatic weapons from a prepared position at nearly point-blank range, and the weight of fire that was poured into the car to realise that the chances of anyone leaving the vehicle alive were zero. Claims that isolated gunshots were heard in the minutes following the initial contact were almost certainly referring to the sounds of ammunition inside the car 'cooking off' in the flames.

The successful removal of the East Tyrone Brigade's premiere assassination team capped off the cycle of tit-for-tat violence that had blighted the Coagh area for more than three years. But the brigade's wider sectarian war continued unabated. In January 1992, members of the East Tyrone PIRA detonated a roadside bomb at the Teebane crossroads near Cookstown. The target was a van carrying civilian construction workers employed at a site on the Lisanelly army base. Eight of the fourteen passengers died, including an off-duty member of the Royal Irish Rangers. The survivors were badly wounded. The fact that all of those killed or wounded were Protestants drew a grimly inevitable response. On 5 February 1992, terrorists belonging to the loyalist Ulster Defence Association burst into a betting shop on the Ormeau Road in Belfast and opened fire on the customers. Five Catholic civilians were killed and nine more wounded.

Shortly after the Ormeau Road shootings, Mid Ulster TCG received intelligence that the East Tyrone Brigade were planning a sophisticated attack on the RUC station in the town of Coalisland, County Tyrone. Earlier flying-column attacks had been planned and led by veteran members of the brigade. However, the devastating losses at Loughgall and the attrition of other senior members in the years since in SAS ambushes had wiped out an entire generation of East Tyrone field commanders. The attack on Coalisland, the TCG learned, was to be led by a much younger man, Kevin Barry O'Donnell, who was just twenty-one years of age.

Despite his youth, O'Donnell was already well known to the intelligence services. Two years earlier, he had been apprehended in London by the Metropolitan Police after the car he was driving was found to be carrying two assault rifles. His trial on terrorism-related charges took place against the acquittal of the Birmingham Six, innocent Irishmen who had served sixteen years in prison after members of the police fabricated evidence of their involvement in an IRA bomb attack. The jury in O'Donnell's case, deliberating the day after the release of the Birmingham Six, chose to believe O'Donnell's claim that he was a peaceful man who had never been a member of the PIRA. Shortly after his return to Northern Ireland, O'Donnell was again arrested, this time for possession of a Rocket Propelled Grenade launcher, but was not convicted. The security services strongly suspected him of involvement in a number of the East Tyrone Brigade's attacks on off-duty UDR personnel between 1990 and 1992.

The intelligence received by Mid Ulster TCG about the impending attack was impressive in its detail. As well as identifying the commander of the operation, the source revealed that the RUC station in Coalisland would be attacked using a DShK machine-gun mounted on the back of a stolen lorry. The 12.7mm DShK is an extremely heavy weapon with a long range and a powerful punch. Often deployed in an anti-aircraft role, the PIRA had successfully used DShKs to bring down a British Army Lynx helicopter in Armagh in 1988 and a Gazelle light helicopter in Tyrone in 1990. Despite the power of the weapon and its impressive size, it was a strange choice for the planned operation: a close-range shooting of a fortified RUC station.

The RUC base was warned of the expected attack and 14 Intelligence Company operators were assigned to mount an intensive covert surveillance operation on O'Donnell and his suspected team. During the surveillance operation, several members of the East Tyrone Brigade were seen leaving cars in the car park of St Patrick's church in the village of Clonoe, two miles from Coalisland. Source intelligence confirmed that the PIRA ASU intended to drive to the church after the attack and use the cars that had been left there to escape.

Reconnaissance of the area around the RUC station in Coalisland was unable to locate a secure ambush position. Coalisland was a small, fervently republican town, full of men and women sympathetic to the goals and methods of the PIRA. The SAS commander, a senior NCO and former member of the Parachute Regiment, judged that a force concealed in the town centre faced too high a risk of being exposed before the attack. Instead, he chose the car park in Clonoe as the location to intercept the PIRA unit. The ambush party, consisting of more than ten uniformed SAS men, took up their positions on 16 February, expecting the attack to take place that night. Other teams of two or three men in civilian clothes and unmarked cars were positioned on the roads nearby to cut off potential escape routes.

Despite the high-quality initial intelligence and the valuable information gathered by the Det's surveillance teams, neither the SAS men in position nor the officers of Mid Ulster TCG had a full understanding of the PIRA plan. Unbeknown to them, early in the evening of the sixteenth, members of the East Tyrone Brigade had called in a delivery order to a Chinese restaurant in nearby Cookstown. When the driver arrived, he was pulled from his vehicle by gun-wielding terrorists. The intimidating figures informed the driver that they had placed a bomb in the back of his van. He was instructed to drive the bomb to the Cookstown RUC station, where he was to leave the vehicle before it exploded. Fortunately, the terrified delivery man panicked when he was stopped at an army checkpoint and informed the soldiers of the threat. On inspection of the vehicle, the bomb was found to be a hoax. Later analysis by RUC Special Branch and the intelligence services concluded that the Cookstown hoax was meant as a diversion to enable a bomb to be exploded at Coalisland. With the defences of the RUC station destroyed or damaged by the explosion, the heavy machine-gun would be able to wreak a potentially devastating fire on the survivors.

In the event, no bomb was used in the attack. At approximately 10.30 p.m., O'Donnell and his men drove the converted truck with the DShK mounted on the rear into the centre of Coalisland, followed by a support car carrying several additional gunmen. Rather than take advantage of the range of their heavy weapon, they stopped the vehicle immediately in front of the RUC station and fired several bursts of tracer fire into the building. While some damage was done to the structure, prior defensive preparations ensured that no casualties were suffered inside the station.

The waiting SAS team heard the confirmation of the attack over the radio and prepared themselves for combat. The expectation was that the flying column would drive straight to the car park at the church in order to switch into their prepared cars and make their escape. It was with considerable surprise, then, that the commander listened to reports from the Det operators shadowing O'Donnell's unit that the vehicles had diverted from the expected route.

In the wake of this unexpected news, the ambush commander came under intense pressure from the SAS men in the cut-off vehicles to change his ambush position, or to at least release some of the satellite cars to intercept the PIRA team. Unwilling to send his forces away piecemeal, or to throw away the carefully organised plan in order to bodge together something new on the road, the commander stood firm. His troops were ordered to maintain their positions and stick to the roles they had been briefed for.

The unexpected behaviour of the PIRA attacking force was the prelude to an act of outrageous youthful bravado that left the observing Det operators stunned. Believing that there was no threat of immediate pursuit, O'Donnell drove his attack team past the house of Tony Doris, the Coalisland commander who had been killed along with Pete Ryan the previous year. Firing their weapons into the air, flashing the lights of their vehicles and shouting, *'Up the 'RA!'*, they presented a scene as far removed from the professionalism of the Derryard attack as could possibly be imagined.

With their victory parade complete, the PIRA men finally set off out of Coalisland and towards the car park in Clonoe, from where they meant to make their escape. The intention was to dismount the DShK, burn the vehicles that had been used in the attack and then depart in the pre-positioned cars. The PIRA team belatedly arrived at the car park around 10.45 p.m. Moments after coming to a halt, the sky lit up with the sudden eerie glow of flares. The SAS commander had sprung his ambush.

The ambush party let loose with a withering burst of fire that immediately cut down three of the terrorists. The driver of the truck was killed before he could leave his seat and two other men, including O'Donnell, were shot as they stood exposed in the rear of the vehicle, trying to remove the DShK. The remaining PIRA men returned fire, lightly injuring an SAS trooper in the exchange. As the SAS teams began to close in, the surviving members of the PIRA force attempted to escape. One man, Sean O'Farrell, managed to evade the initial exchange of fire but was killed by a cut-off group fifty metres away as he tried to escape on foot. Others fled in the support vehicles, which now 'bomb burst' in all directions. One of these vehicles was intercepted by an SAS satellite car that had been keeping watch on the road about a mile away from the ambush site. The SAS men inside engaged the fleeing PIRA vehicle and wounded its occupant, forcing the car off the road and into a hedge. In the follow-up operation, a wounded terrorist was found trying to hide in an adjoining cemetery.

Aidan McKeever, one of the getaway drivers wounded and arrested at the scene, was given a three-year suspended sentence for his role in the PIRA operation. McKeever later sued the British government, claiming that he was unarmed and had been given no opportunity to surrender. In 2011, a UK court upheld his claim and awarded him £75,000 in damages.

The dead men – Kevin O'Donnell (21), Peter Clancy (19), Patrick Vincent (20) and Sean O'Farrell (23) – were among the leading lights of the younger generation of the East Tyrone Brigade. With their deaths, the degradation of the brigade's ability to mount major operations, begun at Loughgall five years previously, was finally complete. Between the spring of 1992 and the announcement of the PIRA's ceasefire on 31 August 1994, Tyrone PIRA killed five more members of the security forces in mortar and gun attacks. However, they were never again able to launch sophisticated operations on the scale of the Ballygawley, Loughgall or Derryard attacks.

The four men killed in the Clonoe ambush were the last terrorists to lose their lives to the SAS in the Northern Ireland Troubles. However, the war was not quite over yet. The SAS were to mount several further major operations in the final years of the conflict.

CHAPTER FOURTEEN

SNIPER AT WORK

THE SAS (1990–97 – II)

In March 1997, Mid Ulster TCG received intelligence from an RUC Special Branch source that an attack was being planned by the East Tyrone Brigade. The target was, once again, the RUC station in Coalisland, now shared as a base by the British Army. The source confirmed that at least two PIRA terrorists would be involved and that a bomb would be thrown.

An SAS team was deployed to respond to the attack. Under-cover soldiers, wearing civilian clothes and in unmarked cars, kept watch on the area around the base. Shortly after half past nine on the night of 26 March, an explosive device containing approximately 1kg of Semtex blew a hole in the perimeter fence of the base. The waiting SAS teams jumped out of their vehicles carrying MP5s and 9mm Browning pistols and moved immediately towards the pair of men who had thrown the bomb. The soldiers fired as they advanced, wounding both of the terrorists. However, before the wounded men could be arrested and handed over to the RUC, the SAS unit found itself hemmed in by an angry crowd of protestors. One of the bombers was able to climb into a car and escape, while the other, more seriously injured by a gunshot to the stomach, was spirited away by members of the crowd.

There were echoes here of the situation that led to the deaths of two British Army corporals at the hands of an enraged crowd in 1988. However, the soldiers in this case were highly trained and well-armed. The question now was not so much whether they could hold off the crowd but whether it would be possible to maintain their own safety without killing anyone. By 1997, the PIRA leadership and the British government were deeply engaged in the Peace Process that would lead the next year to the Good Friday Agreement and the end of the Troubles. The SAS were under strict instructions not to risk derailing the process by killing PIRA terrorists, orders that were responsible for the light injuries sustained by the two bombers and, ultimately, their escape. But while the death of an active terrorist might be damaging for the Peace Process, the killing of civilians, no matter how threatening the situation became, would be certain to collapse the talks. In order to force the crowd back, the encircled soldiers fired into the air and into the ground, keeping the bullets well clear of the feet of those trying to press in on them. The implied threat in the warning shots was enough to keep the crowd at a distance and, a short time later, RUC officers arrived to disperse the gathering using non-lethal ammunition and traditional riot control tactics.

The young man who had been shot in the stomach was Gareth Doris (19), cousin of the Tony Doris killed by the SAS in Coagh, six years earlier. Doris was convicted for his part in the bombing and sentenced to ten years in prison. He was released in 2000 in the aftermath of the Good Friday Agreement. Twenty years after the bomb attack, on 15 December 2017, Paul Campbell appeared before Belfast Crown Court, where he was charged with involvement in the attack, based on DNA evidence found in the car of the priest who had helped the first bomber escape.

Doris and his fellow bomber have the distinction of being the last men shot by the SAS in Northern Ireland. However, one final major operation preceded the end of the war. The roots of this mission stretched back to events that occurred some seven years earlier.

On 30 December 1990, a Royal Marines patrol was operating a checkpoint near a public house in Cullyhanna in South Armagh when a car approached. Inside the vehicle were two members of the PIRA's South Armagh Brigade, Fergal and Michael Caraher. What happened next was to become the subject of heated debate and a criminal trial. It would later be alleged that one of the marines, Lance Corporal Richard Elkington, smashed the driver's window with his rifle and then fired into the car with no lawful justification. It would also be alleged that Elkington ordered a second marine, Private Andrew Callaghan, to fire at the car as well. Fergal Caraher was killed by the gunshots while his brother Michael was badly wounded.

The two marines stood trial for murder in 1993. Lance Corporal Elkington and Private Callaghan claimed that they had opened fire when the Caraher brothers' car tried to force its way through the checkpoint and that they believed it was carrying a third marine away on its bonnet. This defence was remarkably similar to that used on several occasions by SSU teams in the early 1980s. The two marines were acquitted of all charges.

Michael Caraher lost both his brother and a lung in the shooting, but recovered sufficiently to rejoin the South Armagh PIRA, where he became a member of one of its sniper teams. These teams were responsible for the deaths of seven British soldiers and two RUC constables between 1994 and 1997. The elimination of the sniper squads became a top priority for the security forces.*

The PIRA, like most other insurgent organisations, had employed snipers from the very beginning of its campaign. During the Troubles, some 180 British soldiers, policemen and Prison Service officers were killed by PIRA snipers. While snipers could be effective in urban areas such as Belfast and Londonderry, the rural terrain of South Armagh, with its long lines of site and ample cover for concealment, was ideal for such tactics. The South Armagh Brigade used a wide variety of weapons in its attacks, ranging from venerable Second World War vintage weapons, such as the .303 Lee Enfield and the American .30 Garand, to more modern rifles, like the .223 Armalite and the Belgian 7.62mm FN.

---

* The following account of the operations of the Armagh sniper teams is greatly indebted to Toby Harnden's excellent *Bandit Country: The IRA and South Armagh*, London: Coronet Books, 2000.

Snipers working with such weapons could be countered by the Army's own 7.62mm Self-Loading Rifle (SLR), a variant of the FN FAL, which, in the right hands, could hit back accurately out to 600 yards. The SA80, which replaced the SLR from the mid-eighties onwards, was extremely accurate out to 300 yards as an individual weapon and a section firing together could put effective fire on a target out to the same distance as the SLR. Most Army foot patrols operating in South Armagh, especially those from the Parachute Regiment and Royal Marines, also deployed at least one member armed with the L42A1, a converted Second World War-era Lee Enfield No. 4 with a heavy barrel and a telescopic sight. In the hands of a trained marksman, this rifle was accurate up to 800 yards or more.

The ability of the British forces to respond to snipers changed dramatically in the late 1980s and early 1990s when the PIRA acquired a quantity of US-made Barrett M82 and M90 rifles. These deadly rifles, initially designed for the destruction of light vehicles and the penetration of walls, became the weapon of choice for the South Armagh sniper teams. The M82 and M90 are .50-calibre semi-automatic rifles, firing a bullet that is half an inch across and weighs four times as much as a standard 7.62mm round. The Barrett can fling this projectile out to an effective accurate range of two kilometres, with a total maximum range of four kilometres, well beyond the distance at which any weapon carried on foot patrol by the Army or the RUC could return fire.

Despite the long-range potential of the weapon, the PIRA's sniper teams usually took up position much closer to their targets, preferring to maximise the chances of a successful hit. Attacks were carefully coordinated. The Barretts were rare and valuable weapons and the PIRA units that used them took all possible precautions to avoid the loss of their rifles, which would be almost impossible to replace. Scouts were typically employed to ensure that escape routes remained clear and to warn of Army checkpoints. Specially modified vehicles were also used as platforms for the attacks. Gun ports at the rear of the cars enabled the snipers within to shoot from cover while armour plating protected against any return of fire. The use of these cars also ensured that the sniper team could be withdrawn to safety quickly if the need arose. While the team itself usually consisted of four men, many more could be involved in support roles during an operation.

The first successful shot was landed on 16 March 1990, when a round was fired at soldiers manning a vehicle checkpoint. The bullet penetrated the helmet of one of the men and grazed his head, leaving the lucky soldier with only a minor injury. Two years later, Private Paul Turner of the Light Infantry was less fortunate. On 29 August 1992, Turner was shot in the chest and killed while on foot patrol in Crossmaglen, dying instantly. Private Turner was the first soldier to be killed by a Barrett.

The South Armagh PIRA operated two sniper teams, covering the western and eastern parts of the brigade area. The western unit, focusing its activities around the village of Cullyhanna, was led by Frank McCabe, a senior member of the brigade. One of the shooters in McCabe's unit was Michael Caraher.

The sniper teams in South Armagh continued their operations with notable success throughout 1993, using other weapons as well as the deadly Barretts. RUC Constable Jonathan Reid was shot in the back and killed while manning a checkpoint on 25 February. Lance Corporal Lawrence Dickson of the Royal Scots died after being hit in the chest on 17 March. Private John Randall, Duke of Edinburgh's Royal Regiment, was killed at a checkpoint on 26 June. All three were killed using rifles firing a regular 7.62mm round.

In the aftermath of these shootings, Lieutenant General Sir Roger Wheeler, the senior British Army officer in Northern Ireland, stated to the press that catching the PIRA team responsible was a priority for the security forces in the area. The problem General Wheeler faced was a familiar one when dealing with the South Armagh PIRA: a complete lack of reliable intelligence. No human source intelligence at all leaked from within the South Armagh Brigade, despite the intensive efforts of the intelligence services. One MI5 officer lamented to the author that intelligence was so hard to come by that anyone who managed to get a reliable source inside the brigade would be able to 'write his own ticket'. In the absence of reliable human sources, MI5 inserted covert surveillance devices throughout South Armagh in the hope of picking up at least some careless chatter. However, by 1993, none of these technical sources had yielded any reliable information on the activities of the sniping teams.

On 17 July 1993, Lance Corporal Pullin of the Duke of Edinburgh's Royal Regiment was shot in the chest with a single round from a .50 Barrett rifle while patrolling Carron Road in Crossmaglen. The shot was fired from a modified car with the sniper team in the back. PIRA supporters gloated over the killing, erecting a modified 'Men at Work' road sign in Crossmaglen with the silhouette of a gunman and the words 'Sniper at Work'. Barrett rifles were used in three more fatal shootings between July and December 1993, killing RUC Reserve Constable Brian Woods, Lance Bombardier Paul Garrett and Guardsman Daniel Blinco. Guardsman Blinco was shot dead on the anniversary of the killing of Fergal Caraher in 1990. Many in the security forces believe that Michael Caraher was the shooter.

During this time both 14 Intelligence Company and the SAS made several attempts at mounting operations against the Armagh sniping teams. The SAS even deployed its own highly trained snipers to the area in the hope of being able to return fire when an attack happened. However, none of these operations resulted in any tangible results.

On 31 August 1994, the PIRA leadership announced a 'complete cessation of military operations' in order to pursue peace talks with the British government. All PIRA units were ordered to stand down by the Army Council as the strategy pursued by the Adams/McGuinness faction moved towards its culmination. The imposition of the truce caused a rift in the South Armagh Brigade, with many of its members seeing the move as an outright betrayal of everything they had been fighting for. As a result, some abandoned the organisation entirely while others reduced their commitment.

The imposition of the truce was a godsend for the intelligence services. For the first time, 14 Intelligence Company operators could be deployed into South Armagh safely and in large numbers. MI5 were also able to insert new covert listening devices in key areas. By the time the PIRA ceasefire broke down in February 1996, the strength and operational effectiveness of the South Armagh PIRA had been greatly diminished. The reduction of PIRA manpower allowed the Det operators in the area to continue working with greater freedom than had been possible before the ceasefire and paved the way for intensive surveillance operations to be conducted on those suspected of ongoing terrorist activity. Operators identified several farms as possible staging posts for the PIRA sniper attacks. One in particular, near the small village of Freeduff, not far from Crossmaglen, drew particular attention. In order to increase the sources of available data, a team of Det operators was inserted under SAS cover to attach a tracking device to a suspicious vehicle on the farm.

With the ceasefire over, the sniper attacks began again. On 17 February 1997, Lance Bombardier Stephen Restorick of the Royal Horse Artillery was shot dead while manning a checkpoint in South Armagh. The shooting finally gave the intelligence services the break they needed. The tracking device placed on the car outside Freeduff showed that the vehicle had moved from its initial position before the shooting and that it was stationary near the target when Restorick was killed. A close night-time inspection of the vehicle by the Det a few days later confirmed that they had found their quarry: the vehicle was found to have an armoured plate in the boot that could be moved to allow a sniper to fire from within.

Certain now that they had found a location that was used by the sniper team, 14 Intelligence Company mounted a large-scale surveillance operation on the farm, planting cameras and microphones, as well as positioning operators in OPs all around the area. As the comings and goings were monitored over the following weeks, more and more suspected members of South Armagh PIRA were connected to the location.

Those leading the operation hoped that ongoing surveillance on those identified would lead to the exposure of other staging locations. For the moment, though, it was vital to ensure that no further attacks could be carried out from the farm. An SAS response team was put on standby to intercept the sniper team if it seemed that another attack was imminent.

On 10 April 1997, Det operators observed activities that were consistent with preparations for a new attack. The SAS unit was deployed. For the first time in the Northern Ireland conflict, SAS troopers were given strict instructions that they were to interdict an active PIRA unit but were not, 'under any circumstances', to shoot anyone. Peace negotiations were too close to bearing fruit to risk the damage that could be done by killing PIRA members. What followed was the first fight between the PIRA and the SAS that relied on fists and knees alone. With no firearms immediately to hand, the PIRA unit stood little chance. In little more than a minute, James McArdle, Michael Caraher, Bernard McGinn and Martin Mines had been subdued and were prepared to be handed over to the RUC. As McGinn was being led away, anger written across his face, one of the SAS NCOs present tried to console him: 'You don't know how lucky you are. If this had happened a couple of years ago, you'd all be dead.'

In addition to the four members of the sniper team, a Barrett M90 was captured in the operation. Forensic analysis linked the weapon to the shooting of Lance Bombadier Restorick, who was to be the last British soldier killed in Northern Ireland before the Good Friday Agreement. Bernard McGinn confessed to his role in the murder and then went on to give his interrogators a flood of other information. Describing his own PIRA career, he admitted to making explosives on an almost-daily basis in locations on both sides of the border, as well as to having been part of a team that had carried out bombings in England in the late 1980s and early 1990s. He also gave up the names of nearly two dozen members of the South Armagh PIRA, including Frank McCabe, the leader of the unit. While McGinn later withdrew these statements, they proved invaluable to the security forces.

In 1999, McGinn was sentenced to 490 years in prison for his part in dozens of offences, including three bombings in London as well as the killings of three soldiers in Armagh. According to press reports, McGinn laughed out loud when his sentence was announced in court; under the terms of the Good Friday Agreement signed in 1998, he knew he would serve no more than 16 months. Other members of the sniper team were convicted of a range of offences, including six murders. All were set free the following year.

* * *

On Saturday, 19 July 1997, the PIRA announced that a new ceasefire would come into effect at midnight. This time, the ceasefire held, and the following year a comprehensive peace agreement was signed that led, in 2005, to the PIRA disarming and standing down as an armed organisation forever. The focus of the movement now became the pursuit of the republican agenda through the expansion of Sinn Féin's legitimate political power. At the time of writing, Sinn Féin is the largest nationalist party in the Northern Ireland Assembly, with 27 MLAs, and the joint-largest party overall, matching the number of representatives of the Democratic Unionist Party (DUP). Sinn Féin currently holds 37 out of 166 seats in the Dáil Éireann, the Republic of Ireland's lower house, and 5 out of 60 seats in its upper house, the Seanad Éireann. In the 2017 UK general election, Sinn Féin won 7 out of Northern Ireland's 18 seats at Westminster; a number it also won in the general election of 2019. In the last vestige of the abstentionist policy, Sinn Féin MPs do not take up their seats in London, although they do participate in the legislatures of both Northern Ireland and the Republic.

Within eighteen months of the signing of the Good Friday Agreement, the SAS were quietly withdrawn from Northern Ireland. The brief period of global calm at the end of the 1990s was shattered by the attacks on the World Trade Center (WTC) in 2001, and the SAS went on to see intense combat in all theatres of war in the conflicts that followed. 14 Intelligence Company remained in Northern Ireland a little longer. Having been created specifically for service in the province, it looked for a time as if the unit might disappear with the ending of the battle there. Fortunately, forward-thinking individuals in the Ministry of Defence recognised that the skills and institutional knowledge built up over nearly three decades of daily operations were irreplaceable. Instead of being stood down, a new Special Forces unit, the Special Reconnaissance Regiment (SRR), was raised around the core of the Det to provide dedicated surveillance capabilities anywhere in the world. The SRR has since been deployed in all theatres of the so-called Global War on Terror, serving with particular distinction in the conflicts in Iraq and Afghanistan.

In July 2007, the British Army formally ended Operation Banner, the ongoing deployment of troops as part of the security response to the Troubles in Northern Ireland. Lasting thirty-eight years in total, Operation Banner was the longest military campaign conducted by the British Army. According to MoD figures, 763 servicemen died as a result of terrorist activities during the conflict, including serving and former members of the Ulster Defence Regiment who were killed while off-duty. Of the 300,000 troops rotated through deployments to Northern Ireland between 1969 and the end of the conflict, 6,116 were wounded.

The Royal Ulster Constabulary suffered grievously during the Troubles: 314 officers were killed and over 9,000 were injured. In 1999, the RUC was awarded the George Cross in recognition of the collective and sustained bravery of its members and their families, becoming the Royal Ulster Constabulary GC. The only previous such collective award had been granted to the island of Malta for its fortitude throughout the Second World War.

Two years later, on 4 November 2001, in accordance with the terms of the Good Friday Agreement, the RUC was stood down and became the Police Service of Northern Ireland. There is no mention of the George Cross in the new organisation's title. RUC Special Branch, which had done so much to thwart the campaigns of both republican and loyalist terrorists, was disbanded.

CHAPTER FIFTEEN

REFLECTIONS

Important as the PIRA's 1997 ceasefire was, it did not bring an end to terrorist violence in Northern Ireland. Repeating a pattern that had been seen many times before, moves towards peace with Britain led to a fracturing of the republican movement, with dissident hardliners breaking away from the PIRA to form new groups. A little over a year after the ceasefire announcement, a dissident group calling themselves the Real IRA (RIRA) detonated a bomb in Omagh, County Tyrone. Twenty-nine people were killed and hundreds more wounded in the single worst atrocity of the Troubles.

The ferocity of the Omagh attack and the indiscriminate slaughter of civilians might have been unparalleled in the conflict but the number of dissidents involved was small. The Adams/McGuinness faction had achieved a high degree of political cohesion within the PIRA and few were willing to break that unity. With significant concessions by the British government on the table, as well as guarantees that the Republic of Ireland would withdraw its historical claim on the province and affirm the right of the Northern Irish people to choose their own future, a comprehensive majority on all sides of the debate believed that further conflict was futile. However, the small minority who remained dedicated to the ideal of physical force have continued to carry out sporadic acts of violence down to the present day, killing members of the security forces and civilians, as well as brutalising their own communities with a brand of kangaroo justice that relies on beatings and punishment shootings. Dissident groups such as the Real IRA, the Continuity IRA (CIRA) and, more recently, the New IRA (NIRA), have only a fraction of the support and resources that bolstered the Provisional IRA in its heyday. Nevertheless, they still retain the ability to cause significant damage, both to individuals and to community relations more broadly.

In response to the ongoing activities of dissidents in Northern Ireland, members of the Special Reconnaissance Regiment (SRR), the successor unit to 14 Intelligence Company have been redeployed to the province in recent years after a lengthy deployment in distant theatres. SRR operators now continue to carry out the role that an earlier generation of Det men and women originated, working on a daily basis to disrupt both dissident republican organisations and loyalist groupings that have turned to organised crime in the years since the Good Friday Agreement.

* * *

The legacy of the bitter undercover war fought during the Troubles persists to this day. It is clear that mistakes were made by the British security forces at a number of points during the thirty-year history of the conflict, both at the operational level and at the command level. This is particularly true of the early years of the war, during which poor oversight and underdeveloped procedures led to embarrassments, failures and unnecessary civilian deaths. The actions of the MRF, in particular, constitute an indelible stain on the reputation of the British Army.

The legitimate complaints that can be raised against the MRF served to colour perceptions of all future undercover operations. For many republican activists, the pursuit of 'lawfare' against the British government over the conduct of the undercover war has provided a fertile new battleground. A seemingly endless succession of court cases and compensation claims have been pursued in an attempt to delegitimise every single engagement that led to the deaths of PIRA men and women taking part in violent actions. At the same time, dead terrorists who lost their lives while trying to commit murder against normally unarmed targets are lauded as heroes. Distasteful as this narrative may be, it is, perhaps, a necessary step in cementing the peace. A repudiation of the tactics pursued during the Troubles would, when combined with the fact of the PIRA's disarmament, smack too deeply of defeat.

The decision taken by Gerry Adams and Martin McGuinness to guide the movement towards peace was predicated on the realisation that victory through military means was impossible. For a short period in the early 1970s, the PIRA was an insurgent organisation that could fight running gun battles in the streets of Northern Irish cities, that could close off areas to British authority for days or weeks, and that could genuinely threaten the possibility of a major military uprising. The story of the PIRA's ability to fight after the mid-seventies is one of slow but inexorable decline. In the twenty years between 1972 and 1992, the number of soldiers and policemen killed in the province each year dropped from 148 to just 11 (although 1993 was to see a spike to 18 deaths). At the same time, the organisation's ability to mount major operations declined significantly. Arrests and deaths took a clear toll but the most important factor was the ability of the intelligence services, including 14 Intelligence Company, to prevent attacks before they happened.

The murky world of agent handling is one of the most controversial areas of British activity during the Troubles and is a topic upon which the present book has only touched very lightly. The author has no direct experience of the work involved or of the overall strategic approach pursued, only a second-hand understanding acquired through personal contacts with agent handlers from MI5, RUC Special Branch and military intelligence. What is clear is that the infiltration of agents into the PIRA, the INLA and loyalist terrorist organisations shortened the conflict in Ulster considerably. Thanks to the efforts of civilian and military agent handlers, the Belfast and Londonderry Brigades of the PIRA, which had caused so many casualties to the security forces in the early 1970s, were all but neutralised as military forces. Terrorist attacks would still be launched by PIRA units in these two centres throughout the 1980s and 1990s but the scale of activity was an order of magnitude lower than that seen earlier in the conflict.

From an operational perspective, perhaps the greatest achievement of the conflict was the degrading of the East Tyrone Brigade of the PIRA. I have absolutely no doubt that, had it not been for the success of the Loughgall ambush, the East Tyrone Brigade would have broken away from the PIRA and formed a new, more hardline organisation. With dynamic and iconic leaders such as James Lynagh, Seamus McElwaine, Padraig McKearney and Patrick Kelly, this new organisation would have attracted many members from other brigades who resented the PIRA's direction of travel. It is possible that many, if not all of the formidable South Armagh Brigade would have defected as well. With a powerful vision, its own supply of weapons and a dedication to achieving a full-fledged military victory, a 'bandit country' splinter group operating on a flying-column model would have presented an almost insurmountable obstacle to peace if it could not be neutralised. Indeed, the very existence of such an organisation would probably have prevented the PIRA's leadership from pursuing peace negotiations, out of fear that the PIRA would follow the OIRA into irrelevance as all the most active and committed men of violence defected.

While the Loughgall ambush may have been decisive in forestalling this development, it is important to remember that Loughgall was only the first blow in a campaign that spanned five years. The East Tyrone Brigade remained the most active regional unit in the PIRA through to the early nineties. It took a succession of expertly executed ambushes to change this state of affairs. Half of the men the brigade lost during the Troubles were killed between 1987 and 1992, the vast majority dying in SAS ambushes. After the destruction of Kevin O'Donnell's column at Clonoe, the brigade was no longer able to mount sophisticated operations. While isolated shootings and mortar attacks continued, Jim Lynagh's vision had run its course. The degrading of the brigade's capabilities also meant that it was in no position to oppose the PIRA ceasefire in 1994 and the further moves towards peace that followed. That the diminishing of the operational capacity of the brigade served the agenda of an important faction in the PIRA's leadership as much as it did the security forces is the likely explanation for the stream of high-level intelligence upon which the SAS relied during their campaign.

Having lived in Northern Ireland for many years while serving in both the Army and the RUC, my experience of the people of the province is that they are warm-hearted, fiercely loyal to their communities, and that, more than any others I have met, they live with one foot planted firmly in the past. At the time of writing, the past is still a living thing in Northern Ireland. An ongoing inquest is currently examining the events that took place in Ballymurphy in August 1971, during which members of the Parachute Regiment killed eleven people. Two soldiers are currently awaiting trial for murder over the shooting of Joe McCann, a top OIRA gunman, in the Markets area of Belfast in 1972. Other members of the same regiment are waiting to hear whether they will be prosecuted for their part in the events of

Bloody Sunday. At the same time, families whose relatives were 'disappeared' by the PIRA continue to search for answers.

Amidst this retrospective examination of events long past, there are continued calls for new investigations into shootings carried out by both 14 Intelligence Company and the SAS. Claims persist that undercover soldiers were subject to an organised 'shoot to kill' policy, while some also argue that undercover soldiers colluded with Protestant paramilitary organisations. One of my aims in writing this book has been to offer a response to some of the myths that have been generated by the republican propaganda machine and that are still being fed today. I can state quite categorically that no member of the SAS or 14 Intelligence Company was ever specifically ordered to kill any member of an illegal terrorist organisation. Terrorist casualties were the result of a simple but inexorable logic of violence, set in train when someone chose to take up arms in order to murder others and crystallised in the moment of an armed engagement. Once the bullets had begun to fly, the chances of a terrorist successfully communicating that they are no longer any sort of threat were minimal, albeit not entirely zero.

I hope to have shown in these pages that SAS soldiers and Det operators were not unthinking, unintelligent, gun-toting cowboys. Each Special Forces soldier who served in the province was well aware of the political nature of the conflict in which they were involved. They also knew that they had to have the 'moral high ground' when they opened fire. It is a simple fact that the vast majority of PIRA, INLA, IPLO and UVF terrorists killed by the SAS or the Det were both armed and directly engaged in attempts to kill when they died. Republican propagandists, sometimes aided by sympathetic mainstream media outlets, maintain that these heavily-armed and highly dangerous terrorists should have been captured and arrested instead. As I have tried to show by taking the reader through the history of undercover operations in Northern Ireland, it was discovered quite early on that giving advance warnings to armed PIRA terrorists could be lethal for the soldiers involved. The killing of 14 Intelligence Company operator Lance Corporal Jones by PIRA gunman Francis Hughes attests to this. The use of intelligence-led ambushes to interdict terrorist units after they had already begun firing evolved in response to the fatal lessons learned early in the war. It was a highly effective tactic that significantly increased the safety of the soldiers involved.

In the modern fight against Islamic terrorism, British government policy no longer requires that British forces can only kill terrorists if they pose a direct and immediate threat to life. Drone strikes have been used to target British citizens belonging to ISIS/ISIL as targets of opportunity, regardless of the activities the targets were engaged in when struck. The notorious Mohammed Emwazi, better known as 'Jihadi John', was killed the moment actionable intelligence allowed. Most people would, I believe, accept that giving him the benefit of the doubt and waiting until he was within seconds of killing someone before considering him a legitimate target would be unreasonably generous, not to mention dangerous for his potential victims.

Similarly, it is worth considering the way in which armed response units of the Metropolitan Police dealt with the terrorist attack on London Bridge in 2017. On 3 June, three Islamist extremists rampaged throughout the area, stabbing anyone they could find in an attack that left eight civilians dead and dozens more wounded. When armed policemen arrived at the scene, the terrorists were all brought down by gunfire. However, on seeing that one of the terrorists was still breathing and another was slowly moving his arms, the firearms officers present proceeded to shoot each terrorist in the head until all movement ceased. This action, which mirrored many controversial killings in Northern Ireland, would surely have been described by some as a 'cold-blooded execution' if PIRA men had been the targets. In fact, the police officers in London were simply doing their duty to ensure that the men on the ground were unable to cause further harm to those around them. Unsurprisingly, a coroner's court returned a verdict of lawful killing in July 2019.

Few commentators have raised so much as a murmur about whether Jihadi John posed an imminent threat when he was, to quote an American source, 'evaporated'. Fewer still objected to the news that British citizens had been calmly shot in the head by armed police while lying wounded on the ground in London. I believe it is important to ask how, if it is lawful self-defence to kill an Islamist terrorist in Iraq with a drone strike or to neutralise a wounded threat in London, it could have been anything other than lawful self-defence to kill a PIRA terrorist armed with an AK-47, an Armalite or a DShK heavy machine-gun in Northern Ireland?

With regard to claims of 'collusion', while no member of the SAS or 14 Intelligence Company at any point colluded with members of Protestant paramilitary organisations, the same cannot be said for members of the RUC and the UDR. Given the bitterly sectarian nature of the conflict in Northern Ireland, and the fact that the UDR and the RUC were predominantly manned by Protestant Unionists from the region, this is perhaps unsurprising. However, these facts do not excuse such behaviour, which certainly rose on many occasions to the level of the criminal.

Most such collusion was fairly 'low level', with rank-and-file members of the UDR and RUC sharing information with friends or fellow travellers in loyalist organisations. More serious are the questions surrounding the running of agents inside republican and loyalist groups by handlers in RUC Special Branch, MI5 and the FRU. In some cases these agents seem to have been mishandled and allowed access to information they should not have seen. In other cases, there are good reasons to believe that handlers guided both republican and loyalist agents towards attacking specific targets.

The case of Brian Nelson, a former British soldier who became a highly placed intelligence officer in the UDA, provides a clear example of this sort of highly questionable behaviour. Not only did military intelligence officers help Nelson organise the information that the UDA gathered on potential targets, but his handlers also failed to protect at least some potential victims who had been designated as targets by Nelson. At least four of Nelson's targets were later assassinated by the UDA, including the solicitor

Pat Finucane. Nelson was arrested as part of the Stevens Inquiry and claimed in a statement that his handlers had used him to make the UDA more effective in its killing of republicans. When Nelson's case came to court, Colonel Gordon Kerr, the head of the FRU, argued that intelligence gathered by Nelson had enabled the security forces to prevent more than 200 planned murders. Nelson ultimately pleaded guilty to a variety of offences and was sentenced to ten years in prison.

The controversies surrounding Nelson's case give an insight into the difficulties involved in successfully handling a highly-placed agent in a terrorist organisation. There can be no doubt that those who handled agents on both sides of the sectarian divide 'colluded' with them to some degree. However, in assessing this fact it is necessary to consider it from a pragmatic view. In some cases, handlers seem to have attempted to tread an almost impossible moral line by directing their agents' activities onto what they might have thought of as 'acceptable' targets. Given the tit-for-tat sectarian violence that involved, on one side of the equation, PIRA attacks on members of the Protestant community, loyalist revenge killings were inevitable. It is perhaps understandable, if not excusable, that some intelligence officers took the view that it was better for the UDA and UVF to kill actual members of the PIRA and INLA in response, rather than to target innocent Catholic civilians.

The idea that agents within loyalist and republican terrorist groups were allowed to carry out terrorist acts, including murder, is one of the most challenging ethical difficulties to come out of the Troubles. On the one hand, it is clear that colluding in murder in this way can never be accepted or condoned in any civil society, as it is antithetical to everything for which a society of laws stands. On the other hand, if a source is to survive and prosper as a member of a terrorist organisation, then they must appear to others within the organisation as a successful terrorist. It is impractical to suggest that a handler who is running a highly-placed source should insist that the source immediately stop acting as a terrorist, for such a course of action will destroy the value of the agent.

This kind of hard choice is nothing new, and is faced whenever police or intelligence agencies attempt to penetrate criminal or terrorist gangs, or, indeed, whenever it is necessary to make any choice between lesser and greater evils. Still, it is important to reflect upon the challenges it presents and on the grim reality that it is almost impossible to walk away with clean hands once one has first been caught on the horns of the dilemma. Agents such as Nelson in the UDA or 'Stakeknife' in the PIRA's internal security unit were crucial in neutralising the terrorist threat in Northern Ireland. The intelligence each produced saved dozens or hundreds of lives and contributed to ending the Troubles earlier than would otherwise have been possible. Indeed, according to Colonel Kerr, one of those saved from assassination by Brian Nelson's intelligence was none other than Gerry Adams himself. Had Adams been killed as was planned, then the man who was, more than any other, instrumental in pushing PIRA away from violence, would have been unable to force through the changes that led the PIRA to the negotiating table. With Adams out of the picture, we can only guess how much longer the violence would have lasted. But in order for agents to provide this invaluable intelligence, it was necessary that their handlers turned a blind eye to at least some of their illegal activities. Yet in doing so the handlers inevitably compromised their own integrity and that of the government for which they worked.

Agent handling during the conflict in Ulster has aptly been described as a 'Dirty War'. In cases in which handlers knew and allowed agents to carry out terrorist attacks, failed to provide warnings, or even guided terrorists to attack particular targets, those who made those decisions will have to live with their consciences. Only history can really judge their actions as right or wrong on a balance of outcomes, even if those actions must necessarily be judged as morally and legally stained in any case. In finding a way to deal with such moral difficulties as a society, it is useful to reflect on the way in which Britain responded as a nation to the bombing of German cities during the Second World War.* For a long time after the war, there was great reluctance to memorialise the operations of Bomber Command. Bomber Command's business necessarily involved the wholesale killing of civilians in the German cities that were targeted, especially in the 'thousand bomber raids' towards the end of the war. The general sentiment in the aftermath was that, while this aspect of the war might have

---

* For a detailed discussion of the topic, see A.C. Grayling's *Among the Dead Cities: The History and Moral Legacy of the WWII Bombing of Civilians in Germany and Japan*, London: Bloomsbury, 2009.

contributed a great deal to the outcome, it was not something to be celebrated. Rather, it was a guilty act to be borne, a necessary evil that should not be erased and recast as a noble pursuit. A similar approach to the issue of agent handling in Northern Ireland may well be appropriate. And if there are no statues to the men of the intelligence services, no glorification of their actions, this seems only appropriate for those who have always worked in the shadows.

* * *

Northern Ireland today is unrecognisable from the blood-soaked days of its not-so-distant past. The 'peace dividend', combined with generous government subsidies, has paid off by driving the economy forward and lifting many out of the kind of hopeless poverty that fosters extremism. Meanwhile, community relations, while often still tense, are greatly improved. It is safe to say that, while 'peace walls' still divide Catholic and Protestant areas in Belfast, the people of the province are more content, happier and more comfortable in each others' company than at any time in its turbulent past. Without the sacrifice, dedication and bravery of those who took part in the 'Undercover War', none of this would have been possible.

ABOUT THE AUTHOR

Harry McCallion is in a unique position to tell the story of the undercover war during the Troubles. He served seven tours in Northern Ireland with the Parachute Regiment and undertook selection for the secretive 14 Intelligence Company. He completed six years with the SAS, including two tours in the anti-terrorism team, before joining the Royal Ulster Constabulary – where he received two commendations for bravery during six years of service that was ended by a bad car accident. After his career in the police came to an end, he trained in law and is now a successful barrister based in the northwest of England, working in the civil and criminal courts.

His autobiographical book, *Killing Zone*, was published by Bloomsbury in 1995.

Fiction by the author:

Double Kill
Hunter Killer
Ghosts of the Past
Blood Debt

ACKNOWLEDGEMENTS

Without the help of friends, there would be no joy in writing. Many thanks to my friend and copyeditor Paul for his immense professionalism and tireless efforts; also, James Hodgkinson and all the staff at Bonnier Books. Finally, I would like to thank all my friends, both ex-military and civilian, for their continued encouragement and support.